Spelling Matters

Jim Hildyard and Mark Morris

2

Heinemann

Heinemann Educational Publishers
Halley Court, Jordan Hill, Oxford OX2 8EJ
A division of Reed Educational and Professional Publishing Ltd

OXFORD MELBOURNE AUCKLAND
JOHANNESBURG BLANTYRE GABORONE
IBADAN PORTSMOUTH (NH) USA CHICAGO

First published 2000

04 03 02 01
10 9 8 7 6 5 4

ISBN 0 435 10634 1

Original illustrations © Heinemann Educational Publishers 2000
Designed and typeset by AMR Ltd. Bramley, Hants
Illustrated by Art Construction, Mik Brown, Phil Healey, Andy Peters
Printed and bound in Spain by Edelvives

Acknowledgements
The authors and publishers wish to thank the following for kindly granting permission to include
copyright material on page 96:

'Kwik-Fit' logo, used with the kind permission of Kwik-Fit (G.B.) Limited, Edinburgh; 'Kwik Save'
logo, used with the kind permission of Somerfield Stores Limited, Bristol; 'Easi Hire' logo, used
with the kind permission of Easi Hire, Mansfield; 'Kall Kwik' logo, used with the kind permission
of Kall Kwik Printing (UK) Limited, Ruislip, Middlesex.

The Publishers have made every effort to trace the copyright holders, but if they have
inadvertently overlooked any, they will be pleased to make the necessary arrangements at the
first opportunity.

Spelling Matters is designed to improve students' spelling at Key Stage 3. It combines a diagnostic approach with lively activities that can be used with a wide ability range for both whole class teaching and independent study. It ensures structured coverage of the spelling requirements of the National Curriculum and the spelling strands of the word level work in the National Literacy Strategy. *Spelling Matters* addresses the kinds of spelling errors analysed in students' work at KS 3, and identified in *Improving writing at key stages 3 and 4* (QCA, 1999).

Each unit in the **Student Book:**
● outlines unit aims so that students know what they will achieve
● offers clear explanations and examples of spelling rules
● provides lively, accessible activities designed to motivate students
● enables students to check their own progress using self-tests.

The **Teacher's Resource Pack** supports the Student Book by providing:
● answers for the activities and self-tests
● homework activities for each unit.

Diagnostic approach

The diagnostic approach enables students to identify areas of difficulty and work on the units in the book that will best improve their spelling. Students can complete the diagnostic tests in Unit 1 then use the answers and analysis on pages 104–111 to direct them to the units they need to work through. Regular self-tests enable students to check their progress and help direct their own learning.

Accessibility

To ensure accessibility, a 'common sense' approach has been taken to teaching spelling rules to KS 3 students. The coverage focuses on material felt to improve spelling, while not referring to some of the complexities, irregularities and exceptions that could result in confusion.

 The aims of the unit are clearly set out.

 A spelling rule is explained. There may be a small number of exceptions but the rule will be true for most cases.

 Handy hints and tips are suggested to help students improve.

 Warns students about errors to avoid and exceptions to rules.

 Indicates homework activities to be found in the Teacher's Resource Pack.

Adjective Words in **bold italics** are explained in the glossary on page 112.

 Students should use a spelling notebook with the Student Book. This logo indicates that they should make notes at that point.

 Turn to Unit 4 page 37 for more help with root words. Cross-references Where appropriate, these are clearly indicated in the margin.

Contents

Contents

Unit 1: Spelling strategies

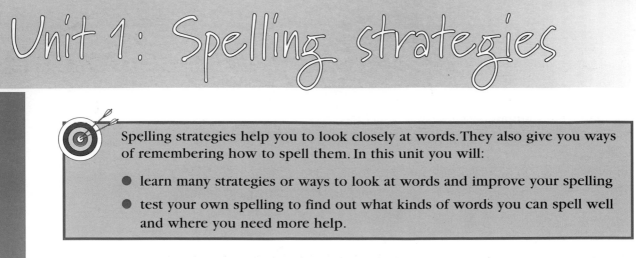

Spelling strategies help you to look closely at words. They also give you ways of remembering how to spell them. In this unit you will:

● learn many strategies or ways to look at words and improve your spelling

● test your own spelling to find out what kinds of words you can spell well and where you need more help.

Look, say, cover, write, check

Use the five steps below to learn how to spell any word. They use sight, sound and memory to help you spell a word you may not have seen before.

1 LOOK	Look carefully at the word for at least ten seconds.
2 SAY	Say the word to yourself.
3 COVER	Cover up the word when you feel you have learned it.
4 WRITE	Write the word from memory.
5 CHECK	Check your word against the original. Did you get it right? If not, what did you get wrong? Spend time learning that bit of the word. Go through the steps again until you get it right.

Activity 1

Choose one of the words below, or a word you know you often spell wrongly. Use the five steps above to make sure you can spell it correctly.

address   friend   necessary

Look, say, cover, write, check

Activity 2

Look back through your own work in English over the last six weeks. Find three words that you often spell wrongly. Use the LOOK, SAY, COVER, WRITE, CHECK steps to help you learn the correct spelling.

Activity 3

Read the article below. Choose three words that you feel are difficult to spell. Use the LOOK, SAY, COVER, WRITE, CHECK steps to learn them.

At the giant radio telescope station, the search for distant alien civilisations goes on. Powerful computers hum as scientists explore the sky for signs of life. But their computers are not enough! They want to use yours, too. As you sleep, they'll work all night, trying to communicate with outer space.

Activity 4

Listed below are some of the most commonly misspelled words in the English language. Complete the challenge below!

Pick a level. The higher the level, the more difficult the words.
1 In pairs, test each other.
2 Use Look, Say, Cover, Write, Check to learn any spellings that you get wrong.
3 When you can spell all the words in that level, WELL DONE! Move on to the next level.
4 When you can spell them all, CONGRATULATIONS on getting 35 of the trickiest words in English right!

Level 1	*1* until *2* knew (to know) *3* friend *4* library *5* sight *6* eight *7* unusual
Level 2	*1* amount *2* videoed *3* necessary *4* exercise *5* receive *6* occasion *7* Wednesday
Level 3	*1* separate *2* sincerely *3* address *4* traveller *5* desperate *6* beginning *7* different
Level 4	*1* independent *2* disappoint *3* beautiful *4* competition *5* definitely *6* excellent *7* noticeable
Level 5	*1* accommodation *2* questionnaire *3* unnecessary *4* government *5* immediately *6* mischievous *7* millennium

Do not try to learn huge numbers of words at once! Seven words are more likely to stick in your head.

Dictionaries and spell-checkers

Use a dictionary to help you spell words correctly. Dictionaries follow the order of the alphabet for grouping words. The guide words at the top of each page show you the first and last word on that page.

Activity 1

Read the notes around this page from a dictionary.

guide word for first entry on the page

indicates how certain letters are pronounced

guide word for the last entry on the page

cheeky   **cherish**

word —— **cheeky** *a.* insolent, saucy.
cheep *v. i.* to utter shrill feeble note as of young bird; *n.* a sound of cheeping.
cheer *n.* 1. frame of mind (stout-hearted, hopeful). 2. shout of encouragement or applause.

chemical (*k-*) *a.* 1. made by, relating to chemistry; *n.* substance obtained by or used in chemical process.
chemist (*k-*) *n.* person skilled in chemistry; dealer in medicinal drugs, also selling other medical goods and toiletries.

second definition, used if a word has one or more meanings

type of word, for example:
*n.= **noun**, a.= **adjective***

indicates slang use of a word

definition

cheesy *a.* 1. like or tasting of cheese. 2.(*sl*) inferior, cheap and nasty.
cheetah *n.* swift-running, spotted animal, can be trained to hunt deer, etc.
chef *n.* man/woman who is head-cook in restaurant, etc.

chequer *n.* pattern made of squares with alternating colours.
cherish *v.t.* protect or look after (child, plant, etc) lovingly; value, hold dear, cling to.

You might find that it helps the 'flow' of your writing if you finish your work before looking in a dictionary to check any words you think you may have spelled wrongly.

Dictionaries and spell-checkers

Activity 2

How do you quickly find in the dictionary two words that start with the same letter? First, find the letter that the word starts with. The words are then listed in alphabetical order by the rest of the letters in the word. For example:

2nd letter	3rd letter	4th letter	5th letter
sang	slant	strange	straddle
sent	sleep	stretch	straggle
sing	slip	string	strap
song	slop	strong	straw
sung	slurp	strung	stray

Write down the following words in alphabetical order:

fade   fire   feather   flint   fiddle   fun   first   feeling   fury   fling

Activity 3

Put these words in alphabetical order. A hidden message will be revealed!

abolish   holidays   June   glorious   ideally
boring   declare   fantastic   all   classes   in

Activity 4

Work in pairs. Open the dictionary in the middle and note down what letter you see. Then one of you says a letter of the alphabet. The other tries to open the dictionary at the correct letter. Score 4 points if you find the letter at your first attempt. If you need two tries, score 3, and score 2 if you need three tries. Score 1 point if you need more than three tries.

Activity 5

All computers have a spell-checker that finds words that have been spelled wrongly. But watch out! Spell-checkers will not find all your mistakes. What are the mistakes in the following sentence? Write it out correctly. Why wouldn't the spell-checker pick them up?

Too people wanted two watch the film, to.

Handheld spell-checkers can be very useful. These help when you don't have a clue how a word is spelled. For example, if you didn't know how to spell **knowledge**, then typing in **nolij** would give you the correct spelling.

Mnemonics

A *mnemonic* is a rhyme or saying that sticks easily in the mind. Use mnemonics to help you to remember how to spell a word.

Activity 1

Read the following mnemonics that a student used to remember spellings. If you have difficulty spelling these words, then learn the mnemonics.

necessary

Never
Eat
Cake
Eat
Salad
Sandwiches
And
Remain
Young

geography

George
Eats
Old
Grey
Rats
And
Paints
Houses
Yellow

separate
Sep**arat**e is **a rat** of a word to spell!

Activity 2

On your own or in pairs, make up two mnemonics that help you remember the following words. If you prefer you could use words you know you often spell wrongly.

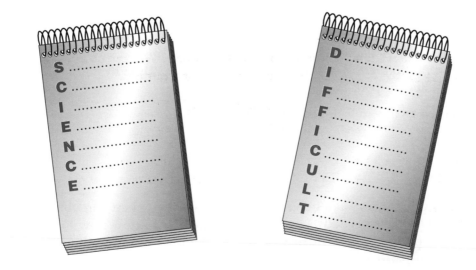

S ....
C ....
I ....
E ....
N ....
C ....
E ....

D ....
I ....
F ....
F ....
I ....
C ....
U ....
L ....
T ....

Saying words as they are spelled

It can help you spell some words if you say them to yourself as they are spelled. In Old English, the **k** of words like *knuckle* was spoken. It would have sounded like *'ke'-nuckle*. People in those times didn't forget to spell it with the **k**.

Activity 1

Read the following report aloud. Pronounce the **k** when it is followed by **n**.

KIDS KNOW BEST!

Research shows that whilst adults knock technology about and kneel in front of the video pushing random knobs, kids kneel down and use their knowledge to knuckle down to recording mum, dad or granny's favourite programme in seconds. Kids, next time you're getting an earful, remember, KIDS KNOW BEST!

Activity 2

Some words have letters that are difficult to hear. It can help you spell the word if you change the way you say it to yourself. For example:

listen	lis / **ten**	say **ten** at the end
interesting	in / **ter** / est / ing	say **ter** in the middle

To help you spell the words below, work out how you will pronounce them. Or you could use three words that you often spell wrongly.

language	library	Wednesday

Breaking words into parts

When you say a word out loud, you can hear that it is made up of one or more beats or sounds called *syllables*. For example, **concentrate** has three *syllables*. It will help you spell a word if you break it into smaller parts.

beat 1	beat 2	beat 3
con	cen	trate

Activity 1

Split the words below into beats or syllables. Write them out with a line between each beat. The first word has been done for you. Learn how to spell the words.

1 mistake = mis / take   *2* improve =   *3* completely =
4 original =   *5* holiday =   *6* development =

Activity 2

Words can often be broken into the following parts. Look at the word **reheated**, for example:

Turn to Unit 4 page 37 for more help with root words.

re	heat	ed
↓	↓	↓
prefix – added to the front of a root	*root word* – cannot be broken up further	*suffix* – added to the end of a root

How many words can you make using the root word **fit** and the prefixes and / or suffixes below? For example, you can make **refitted** and **fitness**.

Prefixes	Root	Suffixes
un		ful
pre		fully
mis		ness
re	fit	ted
out		ter
photo		ting

Compound words

Compound words are complete words made from two root words, for example: **underground**.

Activity 3

How many compound words can you make with the words below? For example you can make **handheld, undergrowth**.

foot	growth	over	play	held	sleep	ground
under	friend	girl	hand		ball	line

12

Letter patterns

Many words contain the same letter patterns. Recognising these patterns will help you to spell more words correctly. There is more about common letter patterns in Unit 5, page 50. For example: wonder**ful**, grate**ful**, beauti**ful** have the **ful** pattern at the end.

There is more about common letter patterns in Unit 5, page 50.

Activity 1

Copy out the table below. Leave some space in each column to add more words later. The table shows letter patterns often used at the start, middle and end of words. Students often spell these letter patterns wrongly.

Word	Start patterns	Word	Middle patterns	Word	End patterns
guess	**gu-**	ch**ie**f	-**ie**-	tau**ght**	-**ght**
physical	**phy-**	trave**ll**er	-**ll**-	wonder**ful**	-**ful**
where	**wh-**	bu**tt**er	-**tt**-	cand**le**	-**le**
wreck	**wr-**	ru**nn**er	-**nn**-	c**ough**	-**ough**
know	**kn-**	co**rr**ect	-**rr**-	ma**tch**	-**tch**
example	**ex-**	ro**bb**ed	-**bb**-	ro**gue**	-**gue**
when	wh-				

Activity 2

Look at the words below. Copy them into the correct place in your table.

when	cu**tt**ing	strai**ght**	ach**ie**ve	**wr**ite
hand**le**	**gu**ard	**kn**ock	horror	ca**tch**
ga**ll**eon	ba**nn**er	sta**bb**ed	**th**ought	event**ful**
bro**gue**	r**ough**	**phy**sics	**ex**cept	

Activity 3

Think of three other words to add to each column of the table that use the same letter patterns.

Proof-reading

Always look over your work for spelling mistakes. If you need to check how a word is spelled, use the LOOK, SAY, COVER, WRITE, CHECK steps to learn it.

With any piece of writing:
- Read your work carefully and underline any mistakes.
- Use a dictionary to check any word you are unsure how to spell.
- You might find it useful to swap work with a partner and look for each other's mistakes.
- If you are working on a computer, use a spell-checker.

Activity 1

Look back at your work in English over the last six weeks. Make a list of the ten spelling mistakes you make most often. Learn how to spell these words using the LOOK, SAY, COVER, WRITE, CHECK steps.

Activity 2

Read the following student's work. The six mistakes have been marked by the teacher. Write down the correct spellings and say what the mistakes have in common.

> sp I made my freind shreik by putting a frog in his sink. I love mischeif
>   and I can catch anyone out if I want to. Last week I caused
> sp greif at home when I told my dad his car had been pinched. He
> sp beleived me as well! It was a peice of genius.

Activity 3

Read the student's work below. Can you find nine mistakes? Write them down with the correct spellings alongside. What common mistake has this student made?

> I grabed a ruber and chucked it at Steve's head. He skiped out
> of the way but he sliped and thuded on to the floor. I was runing
> away grining when I slammed straight into Miss Sutton. She was
> hoping mad and gave me a detention.

A history of words

Activity 1

Read the following article about the history of words.

THE OLD TIMES

price ½ groat

STOLEN WORDS!

English has stolen many words from other languages. For centuries Britain has been a home for Celtic, Viking, Roman, Saxon and French people. All have influenced and changed the language we speak today. Many more words have come into the language through trading with other countries. See next page for details.

DR DICTIONARY

There wasn't even a dictionary until Dr Samuel Johnson wrote one in 1755. Before then, everyone just spelled words as they liked!

(Map showing arrows from Scandinavia, Germany, France, Italy and Greece pointing to Britain.)

Scandinavia

Germany

France

Italy

Greece

Written English 1300 Years Old!

If you tried to read the earliest Old English manuscripts in a museum, you'd find it very difficult! Handwriting, spelling and the English language itself have changed so much that Old English looks like a foreign language now.

Full details on next page …

Still Some Old English Left!

Old English letter patterns still survive today! The most common ones are:

-le   as in catt**le**, ank**le**, bott**le**
-sh   as in fi**sh**, ba**sh**, bu**sh**

Activity 2

Write down the four main things the article tells you about the English language.

A history of words

Did you know?

These words came into English from other languages.

Greek	Latin	Norman French	Norse (Viking)	Saxon
bicycle (with two wheels) hippopotamus (river horse) alphabet (first letters of Greek alphabet: *alpha* and *beta*)	bus (a short form of *omnibus*: for all) motor (mover) doctor (teacher)	parliament (where people talk) courtesy (behaviour at court) beef (bull)	window (wind eye) husband (house-bond: house-owner) herd (from *hyrdir* – shepherd)	Easter (spring religious festival) Lent (spring time) Yule (winter religious festival)

Activity 3

English has been written down for about 1300 years. If it develops for that long again, it will reach the year 3300. What new inventions do you imagine will be around by then? Invent four futuristic things and dream up names for them. Put them in alphabetical order, with brief descriptions.

Activity 4

Read about the following *prefix* which came into the English language from Greek. It comes at the start of many different words and gives a clue to the meaning of a word.

micro (means *small*) + scope (means *see*) = microscope
Definition: A microscope is used to look at small things

micro (means *small*) + phone (means *voice*) = microphone
Definition: A microphone is ...

Write down five other words that use the prefix **micro**. Use a dictionary if you need help.

Activity 5

The table below gives you a prefix (*micro*) and its meaning (*small*).

1 Copy down the table and complete columns 3 and 4.
2 Use a dictionary to find a word starting with each prefix and write down its definition.

Activity 6

Greek prefix	Meaning	Word found	Dictionary definition
micro	small	**micro**scope	
anti	against		
auto	self	**auto**graph	
tele	far		
bio	life	**bio**logy	study of living things
hydro	water	**hydro**electric	

A history of words

The Ancient Greeks did not use the letter **f**. Instead, they used **ph**. Many words in English use the **ph** letter pattern, for example, **ph**one. Complete this quiz by writing out the answers with the missing letter included. All answers contain the **ph** pattern.

1	One of the science subjects.	_ _ y _ i _ s
2	Given as a prize.	tr _ _ _ y
3	Sort of diagram to show data. Line, scatter, bar, are all types of these.	gr _ _ _
4	A famous person's signature	auto_ ra _ _
5	Used for talking over long distances	t _ le _ _one
6	Pictures on a computer screen	gr _ p _ _ cs
7	Taken with a camera	p_ _ togr _ _ h

Activity 7

Can you think of any more words with the **ph** letter pattern? Make up a quiz like the one above and try it out on someone.

If you need more help with **ph** words, turn to Unit 5, page 55.

Activity 8

A French soldier who helped to invade England in the Norman Conquest in 1066, wrote a letter home. Read what he said.

Dear Eloise

I am slowly learning the English language, but it is very hard! They use a type of handwriting called Gothic script. The letter **u** often looks like **v**, **n** or **m**. We keep getting it wrong! So we're changing the letter **u** to **o** in many cases, to make it easier to read. For example:

luve → love   sume → some.

Activity 9

Write down five more words that are spelled with **o** but sound like **u**. Start with welc**o**me.

Activity 10

Create a fact file which includes at least ten of the facts and figures you have learned. Use the title 'Words are history!' or make up a title.

Test your spelling!

This unit has shown you many ways to help improve your spelling. Now use these tests to find out what kinds of spelling you are good at and where you need more help.

Complete the tests below. Then turn to pages 104–111 to check your answers and find out where to go in the book for help.

Don't worry if you don't know all the answers! English spelling can be difficult and many people make mistakes with some kinds of words. Finding out where you need help means you can learn how to get it right.

Diagnostic test 1: Plurals
Write down the plurals of the following words. (Example: *1* **phone** = **phones**)

1 phone	11 elf	21 proof	31 celebrity	41 stimulus
2 wife	12 cigar	22 sundial	32 holiday	42 veto
3 parish	13 goose	23 family	33 handcuff	43 calf
4 loaf	14 valley	24 half	34 church	44 mass
5 studio	15 country	25 video	35 glass	45 schoolboy
6 policeman	16 chef	26 buoy	36 television	46 watch
7 dummy	17 cactus	27 safe	37 cargo	47 oasis
8 clock	18 fax	28 child	38 chief	48 alarm
9 temple	19 tooth	29 kilo	39 sheep	49 stray
10 printer	20 monitor	30 phenomenon	40 factory	50 aircraft

Now turn to page 104 for the answers and where to go for help.

Diagnostic test 2: Spelling and punctuation
These sentences contain spelling and punctuation mistakes. Write each sentence out correctly. (Example: *1* The boy asked, 'Is it Monday today, Joe?')

1 the boy asked, 'is it monday today, joe?'
2 'My make up is running,' cried Andrea.
3 We dont know what he did with Sams shoes.
4 The girls changing rooms were left in a terrible mess.
5 I think i would like to work for the rspca.
6 julie and richard went to spain at easter.
7 You and i should watch friends on tv tonight.
8 I'm going to do alot of work to day.
9 Im going to Petes after school. Youll miss out if you dont come.
10 All most everyone thinks the treasure is in side the pyramid.
11 He has spent a record breaking amount of time in the re-serves.
12 Jane said, 'you really Should learn to Spell properly.'
13 Youre all daft if youre going there. Were staying right here.
14 The dogs going crazy, itll bite you.
15 'The motor way was abit busy this morning,' said Alan.

Now turn to page 105 for the answers and where to go for help.

Test your spelling!

Diagnostic test 3: Homophones, silent letters, Americanisms and deliberate misspelling

Write out the following sentences using the correct spellings.
(Example: *1* It's plain to see that everyone is here now.)

> *1* It's plane to sea that everyone is hear now.
> *2* I onestly think I've recked my nuckles; I think they're broken.
> *3* I'm not sure weather he was board or not.
> *4* I'm in your det because you cured my neumonia.
> *5* The plate will brake if it falls of the table.
> *6* Have you scene the park? The circus is their this weak.
> *7* Which color would you like? Orange, gray or blue?
> *8* I no that I need too work hard on my spelling.
> *9* I didn't realize your behavior could be so awful.
> *10* It's because I'm Krazy that I'm going to give u my money.
> *11* Did we win or loose the 400 meters relay?
> *12* It would be easi to take the kwik route.

Now turn to page 106 to check for the answers and where to go for help.

Diagnostic test 4: Soft letter sounds

Write down the correct spelling. (Example: *1* face)

1 fase / face	*11* sauce / sause	*21* lardge / larj / large
2 palace / paliss	*12* mouce / mouse	*22* bridge / brij / brige
3 genius / jenius	*13* plase / placc	*23* damaj/damadge/damage
4 cylinder / sylinder	*14* furnace / furniss	*24* justice / justiss
5 poultice / poultiss	*15* city / sity	*25* agency / agensy
6 maccive / massive	*16* hice / hiss	*26* cymmetry/symmetry
7 bilge / bilje	*17* cingle / single	*27* range / ranj / ranje
8 sigar / cigar	*18* gewel / jewel	*28* incinerator / insinerator
9 mice / mise	*19* surgeon / surjeon	*29* symbol / cymbol
10 blice / bliss	*20* pensil / pencil	*30* jiraffe / giraffe

Now turn to page 107 for the answers and where to go for help.

19

Test your spelling!

Diagnostic test 5: Common letter patterns

Write down the correct spelling. (Example: *1* vein)

1 vein / vien	*11* weird / wierd	*21* stuffing / stuphing
2 sceince / science	*12* society / soceity	*22* gruph / gruff
3 piece / peice	*13* typhoon / tyfoon	*23* thieves / theives
4 cieling / ceiling	*14* wieght / weight	*24* fanceid / fancied
5 fotocopier / photocopier	*15* species / speceis	*25* graffic / graphic
6 agencies / agenceis	*16* deceive / decieve	*26* freight / frieght
7 phuture / future	*17* orfan / orphan	*27* feild / field
8 ancient / anceint	*18* their / thier	*28* hurried / hurreid
9 beleive / believe	*19* shield / sheild	*29* view / veiw
10 triumph / triumf	*20* greive / grieve	*30* reprieve / repreive

Now turn to page 108 for the answers and where to go for help.

Diagnostic test 6: Common letter patterns

Write down the correct spelling. (Example: *1* echo)

1 echo / ecko / eko	*17* count / cownt	*32* worden / warden
2 pach / patch	*18* broun / brown	*33* worp / warp
3 churtch / church	*19* charade / sharade	*34* swich / switch
4 courage / curage	*20* wreched / wretched	*35* ditch / dich
5 groul / growl	*21* sketching / skeching	*36* technical / tecknical / teknical
6 broshure / brochure	*22* monarch / monark / monarck	*37* opake / opaque
7 which / whitch	*23* brusque / brusk	*38* fake / faque
8 attatch / attach	*24* shandelier / chandelier	*39* question / qestion
9 clowt / clout	*25* shandy / chandy	*40* was / wos
10 cushion / cuchion	*26* huch / hutch	*41* chemichal / chemical / cemichal
11 rich / ritch	*27* much / mutch	*42* catching / caching
12 what / whot	*28* double / duble	*43* quolify / qualify
13 squobble / squabble	*29* ploump / plump	*44* spouse / spowse
14 yung / young	*30* cloud / clowd	*45* reqire / require
15 quolity / quality	*31* shower / shouer	
16 warble / worble		

Now turn to page 108 for the answers and where to go for help.

Test your spelling!

Diagnostic test 7: Prefixes and suffixes

Write out the word and <u>underline</u> the **prefix** (e.g. <u>un</u>known)

1 unknown
2 underground
3 preview
4 impossible
5 misbehave
6 overhead
7 misspell
8 unnecessary
9 antidote
10 disagree

Write out the word and <u>underline</u> the **suffix** (e.g. friend<u>ship</u>)

11 friendship
12 brightest
13 mixing
14 involvement
15 usesless
16 sharpen
17 destroyed
18 lower
19 darkness
20 reported

Write down the correct spelling (e.g. although)

21 allthough / although
22 misbehave / missbehave
23 unatural / unnatural
24 ilegal / illegal
25 misspent / mispent
26 overrule / overule
27 imature / immature
28 unoticed / unnoticed
29 irregular / iregular
30 immediate / imeadiate

Write down the correct **suffix** (e.g. dark<u>ness</u>)

31 dark (ness, ful, less)
32 bright (ing, ly, ful)
33 appoint (ance, y, ment)
34 point (ness, ed, ful)
35 interest (ly, ing, ship)
36 tune (ful, ment, ly)
37 exact (ous, ly, ful)
38 find (ing, ed, est)
39 forgive (less, ness, ship)
40 carry (ing, ly, ful)

Write down the stem word and the **suffix** together correctly (e.g. attractiveness)

41 attractive + ness
42 lady + es
43 amuse + ed
44 playful + ly
45 forgive + ing
46 heavy + est
47 price + less
48 nurse + ing
49 sharp + est
50 force + ed

51 marry + ing
52 ability + es
53 slob + ish
54 wet + er
55 cancel + ing
56 travel + ing
57 care + less
58 hope + ful
59 control + ing
60 spiral + ing

Now turn to page 109 for the answers and where to find help.

Test your spelling!

Diagnostic test 8: Word endings

Make a complete word by adding the correct ending.
Choose from: -tion -sion -ssion -cian. (Example: *1* televi<u>sion</u>)

1 televi	*7* ver	*13* progre	*19* opti
2 magi	*8* techni	*14* distribu	*20* ac
3 adora	*9* profe	*15* confe	*21* politi
4 admi	*10* vi	*16* electri	*22* po
5 expre	*11* aggre	*17* musi	*23* explo
6 revi	*12* emo	*18* occa	*24* promo

Choose from: -ous -ious -eous. (Example: *25* fabul<u>ous</u>)

25 fabul	*30* advantag	*35* hid	*40* myster
26 ser	*31* caut	*36* ambit	*41* simultan
27 gener	*32* marvell	*37* gorg	*42* spontan
28 courag	*33* nerv	*38* fam	
29 superstit	*34* obv	*39* danger	

Choose from: -le -al. (Example: *43* decim<u>al</u>)

43 decim	*49* surviv	*55* residenti	*61* dimp
44 manu	*50* person	*56* memori	*62* fidd
45 purp	*51* mudd	*57* materi	*63* crad
46 bott	*52* miner	*58* stubb	*64* funer
47 fin	*53* comic	*59* mirac	*65* sensib
48 bubb	*54* emotion	*60* critic	*66* benefici

Choose from: -ate -ite. (Example: *67* indic<u>ate</u>)

67 indic	*72* irrit	*77* imperson	*82* navig
68 favour	*73* oppos	*78* celebr	*83* evapor
69 narr	*74* complic	*79* altern	*84* demonstr
70 anim	*75* est	*80* cooper	
71 gran	*76* defin	*81* particip	

Choose from: -ical -icle -acle. (Example: *85* phys<u>ical</u>)

85 phys	*90* art	*95* part	*100* chem
86 mag	*91* ic	*96* mus	*101* spect
87 cub	*92* pract	*97* bibl	*102* class
88 veh	*93* tent	*98* mir	
89 astrolog	*94* log	*99* vert	

Choose from: -ance -ence. (Example: *103* lic<u>ence</u>)

103 lic	*107* excell	*111* appli	*115* experi
104 insur	*108* disturb	*112* sci	*116* perform
105 resid	*109* coincid	*113* ambul	*117* rom
106 sent	*110* brilli	*114* audi	*118* depend

Now turn to page 110 for the answers and where to find help.

Test your spelling!

Diagnostic test 9: Letter patterns

Choose the correct letter pattern to complete each word below.

(a) (ai) (ay) (ei) (ey) (ea)	
1 hurt	= p__n
2 means 'forever'	= alw__s
3 do as you're told	= ob __
4 heavy	= w__ghty
5 wonderful	= gr__t
6 trouble	= d_nger
7 to destroy	= br__k

(e) (ea) (ee) (ie) (ei) (i)	
8 to yell	= scr__m
9 to finish	= compl_te
10 another name for roof	= c__ling
11 to trust	= bel__ve
12 a surprise pleasure	= tr__t
13 road	= str__t
14 washes clothes	= washing mach_ne

(i) (y) (ie) (ye) (uy) (ey)	
15 to break with teeth	= b_te
16 what you see with	= __e
17 farewell	= goodb__
18 to purchase	= b__
19 to colour fabric	= d__
20 not tell the truth	= l__
21 certain kind	= t_pe

(o) (oa) (ow) (ough) (ew)	
22 you drive on it	= r__d
23 to possess	= __n
24 not fast	= sl__
25 dogs like these	= b_nes
26 type of ship	= b__t
27 to stitch	= s__
28 bread is made from it	= d____

(u) (oo) (o) (ew)	
29 to misplace	= l_se
30 month of the year	= J_ne
31 bad-mannered	= r_de
32 you eat with it	= sp__n
33 staff of a ship	= cr__
34 for washing hair	= shamp__
35 PC	= comp_ter

(u) (ue) (ew) (eu)	
36 day of the week	= T__sday
37 student	= p_pil
38 melody	= t_ne
39 not many	= f__
40 female sheep	= __e
41 not taking sides	= n__tral
42 a continent	= __rope

Now turn to page 111 for the answers and where to find help.

Now you have completed these tests, WELL DONE!

Remember that you should check against the answers on pages 104–111 to find out where you are good at spelling. You can also see where to turn in the book to make your spelling even better!

Unit 2: Vowels and consonants

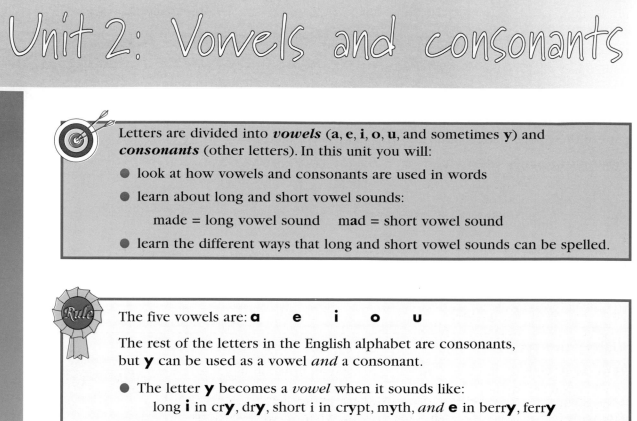

Letters are divided into **vowels** (**a**, **e**, **i**, **o**, **u**, and sometimes **y**) and **consonants** (other letters). In this unit you will:

● look at how vowels and consonants are used in words

● learn about long and short vowel sounds:

made = long vowel sound   mad = short vowel sound

● learn the different ways that long and short vowel sounds can be spelled.

The five vowels are: **a   e   i   o   u**

The rest of the letters in the English alphabet are consonants, but **y** can be used as a vowel *and* a consonant.

● The letter **y** becomes a *vowel* when it sounds like:

long **i** in cr**y**, dr**y**, short i in cr**y**pt, m**y**th, *and* e in berr**y**, ferr**y**

● The letter **y** is a *consonant* when it sounds like:

y in **y**ellow or **y**awn

Activity 1

You can see how important vowels are by looking at the sentences below. All the vowels have been taken away. Fill in and write out the completed passage. (Clue: It is about a very popular national game!)

Th_ f_rst m_tch _f th_ s_ _s_n w_s _b_nd_n_d d_ _ t_ _ t_rr_bl_ h_ _lst_rm. Tw_ pl_y_rs w_r_ _nj_r_d wh_n th_y w_r_ h_t w_th g_lf b_ll-s_z_d l_mps _f _c_.

Vowels can sound long or short.

● A **long vowel** makes the same sound as when you say the name of the vowel: m**a**te   h**e**re   b**i**te   d**o**ze   f**u**se

● A **short vowel** doesn't make the same sound as when you say the name of the vowel: m**a**t   h**e**n   b**i**t   d**o**t   f**u**ss

Short vowels

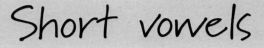

When you hear a short vowel sound in a short word, it is usually spelled with only one vowel:

pat   pet   pit   pot   pub

Activity 1

Write down the **short vowel** words you can make from the following letter grids. Each word must contain the vowel in the centre square.

t	p	r
s	a	b
j	n	c

f	n	t
p	i	l
d	g	b

Activity 2

Sometimes a short vowel sound is made from more than one vowel. The vowels that make the sound may not be what you expect! Copy out the table below. Then say to yourself each word beneath the table. Put each word into the correct column.

short 'e' sound as in bed	short 'i' sound as in bid	short 'o' sound as in box	short 'u' sound as in bud, bull
said	crystal	because	love, good

head   mystery   cough   mother   friend   enough   should   pretty
leisure   book   guessing   was   squad   swan   busy

Activity 3

Write out the following report. Complete the words with letters that make a short vowel sound. Look back at Activity 2 if you need help.

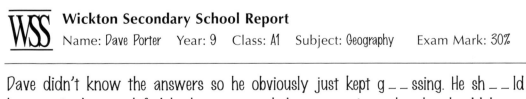

WSS   **Wickton Secondary School Report**
Name: Dave Porter   Year: 9   Class: A1   Subject: Geography   Exam Mark: 30%

Dave didn't know the answers so he obviously just kept g _ _ ssing. He sh _ _ ld have revised more. I feel he has too much l _ _ sure time when he should be sticking his nose in a good old-fashioned b _ _ k. He didn't get a g _ _ d mark bec _ _ se he didn't work hard en _ _ gh. It's a m _ stery to me, because it's cr _ stal clear he is capable when he puts his mind to it. Dave is always b _ sy with something other than his school work.

Long vowel sound 'a'

Long vowels

A long vowel sound can be made by a vowel on its own:

h**a**te th**e**se h**i**re h**o**pe h**u**ge

A long vowel sound can also be made using two or three common letter patterns. For example, the long vowel sound **a** in made can also be spelled:

m**ai**d m**ay** m**ai**d m**ay**

Learning the letter patterns for each vowel sound will help you spell more words correctly.

Activity 1

Copy out the table below and learn these letter patterns that make the long vowel sound **a**. You can see from the table whether the letter pattern is used often or not. Leave enough room to add more words later.

Letter patterns that make the long vowel sound 'a'						
Letter pattern	a (often)	ai (often)	ay (often)	ei (not often)	ey (not often)	ea (not often)
Example	m**a**de	afr**ai**d	pl**ay**	w**ei**ght	gr**ey**	st**ea**k

Activity 2

Read the review below. Put the words with the long vowel sound **a** in blue into the correct column of the table you made in Activity 1.

We review ... Cave Raider IV

If you thought the last three were hard, try this one for size! One of the most difficult strategy games ever made. You'll be playing this one till Doomsday. Eight compact discs means 336 levels of impossibly difficult puzzles, traps and 3D graphics that will make your eyes pop out. Great value for money. We thought they couldn't make a game any better than the last one ... We were wrong.
Afraid it'll beat you? It probably will! Obey your instincts – BUY IT NOW!!!

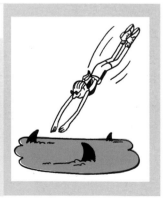

Activity 3

Write your own exciting review of something on sale in the shops, using words that contain the long vowel sound **a**. Try to use each way of spelling the long vowel sound **a** at least once.

Long vowel sounds 'e' and 'i'

Activity 1

Copy out the table and learn these letter patterns.

Letter patterns that make the long vowel sound 'e'					
Letter pattern	e (often)	ea (often)	ee (often)	ie (not often)	ei (not often)	i (not often)
Example	these	please	three	chief	ceiling	machine

Activity 2

Read the article below. Put the words with the long vowel sound **e** in blue into the correct column of the table you made in Activity 1.

The Skyfox parachute team often jump out of planes at 20 000 feet. These youngsters seem to be fearless, even jumping over ravines! Are they weird? The chief instructor agreed to be interviewed. He said: 'We achieve success by being calm. We might feel like screaming but we never do. My team are the bravest there is.'

Activity 3

Copy out the table and learn these letter patterns.

Letter patterns that make the long vowel sound 'i'					
Letter pattern	i (often)	y (often)	ie (often)	ye (not often)	uy (not often)	ey (not often)
Example	fine	type	die	goodbye	buy	eye

Activity 4

Read the recipe below. Put the words with the long vowel sound **i** in blue into the correct column of the table you copied out in Activity 3.

This dish will make you sigh with delight. Friends will fight for a bite. Read on ... It's no lie, it's not just hype. Buy your pumpkin today!

My Traditional Pumpkin Soup

Why not serve this on Halloween night?

Soak one large pumpkin in wine, place on a low heat. Add one shy toad and two bluebottle eyes. Simmer, then drop in one juicy fly. Bring to boil and add 1 pint of dry sherry and ½ cup of blood or red dye. Serve, with a handful of finest straw from a pig sty. Enjoy!

Activity 5

Write a favourite recipe using words containing the long vowel sound **i**.

Long vowel sounds 'o' and 'u'

Activity 1

Copy out the table and learn these letter patterns.

Letter patterns that make the long vowel sound 'o'				
Letter pattern	o (often)	oa (often)	ow (often)	ough (not often)	ew (not often)
Example	go	road	show	although	sewn

The words below all have the long vowel sound **o**. Write them in the correct column of the table you have made. Can you think of any more? Add them to your table.

> toad   bone   explode   unload   approach   soaked   boast
> boat   below   grow   low   dough   goat   throw   though

Activity 2

The long vowel **u** can sound like **oo** (**ru**de) or **yoo** (**cu**be). Copy out the tables below. Learn which letter patterns make each sound.

Letter patterns that make the long vowel sound 'u' (as in rude)			
Letter pattern	u (often)	oo (often)	o (often)	ew (not often)
Example	rude	spoon	do	screw

Letter patterns that make the long vowel sound 'u' (as in cube)			
Letter pattern	u (often)	ue (not often)	ew (not often)	eu (not often)
Example	fortune	Tuesday	few	neutral

Read the review below. Put the words with the long vowel sound **u** in blue into the correct column of the tables you have made.

> Tuesday 14th June   Channel 6, 2.30–3.45pm
> **The Future Squadron**   Rating ✔✔✔
> *Many argue that this afternoon's film is the future of animation. Those who grew up watching crude cartoon buffoons will conclude that there are few similarities. You won't feel neutral about this film! This reviewer approves, will you? Watch out for the new special effects used during the flight to the moon sequence.*

Different vowel sounds: self-tests

Complete the tests below. When you have finished, your teacher will have the answers to check against.

Self-test 1
Write down whether each word has a long vowel sound or a short vowel sound.

1 **Bu**zz short: 'u'
2 **Rea**ch
3 t**i**n
4 str**aigh**t
5 sk**y**
6 cockr**oa**ch
7 p**ay**

Self-test 2
Write down which long vowel sound is made by the letters in bold.

1 I really love st**ea**k. long: 'a'
2 I really h**a**te ch**ee**se.
3 That's a powerful comp**u**ter.
4 Mach**i**nes don't have emotions.
5 Don't worry about me, I'm f**i**ne.
6 I'm not in any d**a**nger, am I?
7 I'm up in the cr**ow**'s nest.

Self-test 3
The answers to the clues below have letters missing. Choose the correct letter pattern for each gap from those given in bold above each set of clues.

Long vowel sound 'a'		
a ai ay ei ey ea		
1 out of the sun		sh**a**de
2 carry food on it	tr_ _	
3 to say 'well done!'	pr_ _ se	
4 do as you are told	ob _ _	
5 smash	br _ _ k	
6 cargo on train/ship	fr_ _ ght	

Long vowel sound 'e'		
e ea ee ie ci i		
7 trick or …	tr _ _ t	
8 put shoes on your …	f _ _ t	
9 be given something	rec _ _ ve	
10 succeed	ach _ _ ve	
11 not there, but …	h _ re	
12 girl's name	Paul _ ne	

Long vowel sound 'i'		
i y ie ye uy ey		
13 colour some material	d _ _	
14 not low	h _ gh	
15 use it to see with	_ _ e	
16 insect	fl _	
17 a penny for the …	g _ _	
18 eat it with chips	p _ _	

Long vowel sound 'o'		
o oa ow ough ew		
19 knead, for bread	d _ _ _ _	
20 got a cold and a sore …	thr _ _ t	
21 not high	l _ _	
22 smashed	br _ ke	
23 mend clothes	s _ _	

Long vowel sound 'u' (oo as in cube)		
u oo o ew		
24 after midday	aftern _ _ n	
25 colour	bl _ e	
26 people who work on a ship	cr _ _	
27 want something to …	d _	

Long vowel sound 'u' (yoo as in tune)		
u ue ew eu		
28 have an angry row	arg _ _	
29 not on anyone's side	n _ _ tral	
30 melody	t _ ne	
31 female sheep	_ _ e	

WELL DONE for the answers that you got right! If you got any wrong, go back to the part of the unit that will help you. Work through the activities again until you get them right.

Unit 3: Plurals

This unit will help you to spell **plural** words correctly. By the end of this unit you will:

- know the many ways to turn **singular** words into plurals
- spell plural words correctly.

Clues Hints Tips

Singular means there is only one: for example, one computer.
Plural means there are more than one: for example, five computers.

When to add 's' or 'es'

Rule

- The most common way to make a word plural is to add **s**, for example:
  book → book**s**

- But there are times when you should add **-es** to make a plural. If a word ends in **s**, **ss**, **sh**, **ch**, **x**, **z** or **zz**, add **-es** to make it plural:

  ben**ch** → bench**es**   di**sh** → dish**es**   hoa**x** → hoax**es**

  You can hear an **-es** plural because it adds another **syllable** to the word. For example:
  bus *(one syllable)*   → bus/es *(two syllables)*
  ad/dress *(two syllables)* → ad/dress/es *(three syllables)*

Activity 1

Read the article below. Write out the words in blue in their plural form.

Stud up! Student left out in the cold

After several clash with teacher, seven pupil from Ashton School have been told to remove their body stud and ring or stay away from school. Four girl and three boy all received letter from the Chair of Governor telling them body piercing is not allowed in nose, mouth, or eyebrow. Only ear lobe are acceptable. Headteacher Victoria Wilkes admitted to a few hitch with the school dress code. 'We respect the wish of our parent. School have uniform because people want them. We've had dozen of message of support. I've got box full of them. This dangerous trend is taking attention away from our many success.' Student Alan Burton said, 'This stuff about risk and danger had us all in stitch. It's rubbish. Pierced ear are just as dangerous. What about kid who've got stud where you can't see them? What if it's part of your culture?' The problem seem set to continue for some time.

30

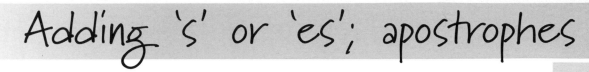

Adding 's' or 'es'; apostrophes

Activity 2

Design a newspaper advertisement for 'Pete's Pet Products' to sell the goods listed below. It must contain each blue word in its plural form.

> aquarium   hutch   kennel   **rodent**   cage   basket   **insect**   tank
> **dog and cat** lead   **vitamin** tablet   **grooming** brush   **food** bowl
>
> **exotic birds our speciality:** parrot   bullfinch **and** goldfinch   macaw
> falcon   albatross   budgerigar   pelican   ostrich   thrush
>
> **unusual animal:** spider   cockroach   ferret   fox   snake   crocodile   goat

Using apostrophes correctly

Simple plurals do not require an apostrophe. It is a mistake to add an apostrophe before an **s** when you mean the word to be a simple plural.

ten spiders ✔   **not**   ten spider's ✘

See Unit 7, page 83 for more on apostrophes

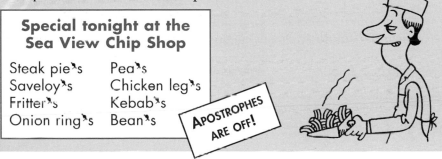

Special tonight at the Sea View Chip Shop

Steak pie's   Pea's
Saveloy's   Chicken leg's
Fritter's   Kebab's
Onion ring's   Bean's

APOSTROPHES ARE OFF!

Activity 3

A student had trouble with plurals and apostrophes. Read what they wrote. Make a list of their twelve mistakes.

> Two week's ago, I bought three new computer game's with the money I saved from doing odd job's. I'm a bit of a computer freak, actually. I've got loads of game's and I'm brilliant at them. This causes me problem's, though, because none of my mate's will play them with me. They don't like the joke's I make when I thrash them. Now they make excuse's like, 'I've got to walk my Gran's dog's' or, 'My girlfriend's coming round', or something like that. Mum's a bit worried because she thinks it's bad if I don't have ton's of mate's, but I don't care. As long as I've got my game's, I'm happy!

Words ending in 'f', 'ff' or 'fe'

- Any words that end in **ff** need an -s to make them plural, for example:
   sheriff → sheriffs   cuff → cuffs

- Words that end in **f** or **fe** are more tricky. Some are made plural by adding **-s**, such as:
   chief → chiefs   reef → reefs

   - Other words ending in **f** or **fe** change the **f** to **v** and add **-es**, such as:
     wife → wi**ves**   leaf → lea**ves**   calf → cal**ves**

   - Some words that end in **f** can be spelled with either an **-fs** or a **-ves** plural ending, such as:
     scarf → scar**fs** or scar**ves**   hoof → hoo**fs** or hoo**ves**
     dwarf → dwar**fs** or dwar**ves**   handkerchief → handkerchie**fs** or handkerchie**ves**

There is no clear rule for how to spell the plural form of a word ending in **f** or **fe**. If you are unsure, always check in a dictionary, and use one of the strategies in Unit 1 to help you learn how to spell it.

A tip that often works is saying aloud the plural of a word ending in **f**. If you can hear a **v** sound, it usually means the plural ends in **-ves**, for example:

   cli**ff**s = **f** sound   cal**ves** = **v** sound

Activity 1

Read the story below. Write down the words in blue in their plural form.

Feeling terrified, Dan looked out of the window towards the cliff. The howling of wolf had woken him but all he could see were leaf falling on the roof of nearby houses. He knew the werewolf were coming to get him but no one shared his belief. He reached up on to the shelf above him and grabbed one of his penknife. It did not make him feel much safer.

Activity 2

Write an account of a nightmare. In their plural form, use as many words ending in **ff**, **f** and **fe** as you can.

Words ending in 'y'

Rule

- If a word ends in a *vowel* before the y, just add **s**, for example:

  d**ay** → day**s**   t**oy** → toy**s**   k**ey** → key**s**

- If a word ends in a *consonant* before the y: change the y to **i**, then add **es**, for example:

  la**dy** → lad**ies**   par**ty** → par**ties**   bul**ly** → bull**ies**

Activity 1

Read the following advertisement. Write down the words in blue in their plural form.

Make your barbecue buzz with our brilliant bargains!

Great buy at Tesway

Double bonus points on all turkey, curry, and chutney!
Ice lolly, Danish pastry, French fry, cherry, strawberry and many different flavoured jelly and ice creams all at 10% off.
All brandy, sherry, chardonnay and lagers from a wide range of brewery - buy one, get one free!

Also! This week only: all food for baby at 20% off.

Why not visit our Garden Centre?

Hundreds of different flower variety: poppy, pansy, daisy, ivy and lily.
Family will enjoy our ANIMAL AREA: see the goats, donkey, pony, and spectacular display of butterfly and canary.

For barbecues, party, and those last minute hurry and scurry, no delay are recommended - only 3 day left ...

visit Tesway WHILE STOCKS LAST!

Activity 2

Write a short article for a school magazine about a school play. Include as many of the following words as possible, in their plural form.

| display | fly | trolley | reply | identity |
| jockey | baby | convoy | story | spy |

Words ending in 'o'

- If a word ends in **o**, it usually needs an **-s** to make it plural, such as:

  disco → disco**s**   shampoo → shampoo**s**

- But some words ending in **o** need an **-es** to make them plural, such as:

  potato → potato**es**   mosquito → mosquito**es**

Clues Hints Tips

There is no clear rule about how to spell the plural of a word ending in **o**. If you are unsure, always check in a dictionary, and use one of the strategies in Unit 1 to help you learn how to spell it.

You could group words that end in **-oes** together in a sentence and learn it:

> Eating too many mangoes, tomatoes and potatoes will make you sick!

Activity 1

Write a newspaper headline for each of the words in blue, using its plural form. Use a dictionary if you need help. For example:

See plurals
Self-test 2,
page 36

COUNCIL TO CLOSE DISCOS SHOCK!

disco   piano   echo   rhino   video   hero   volcano

No change plurals

Clues Hints Tips

Some words are spelled the same whether they are singular or plural:

aircraft   deer   fish   salmon   series   sheep

Activity 2

As there are no rules to help remember no change plurals, write them in your spelling book. Learn them, and get someone to test you.

Irregular plurals

Irregular plurals are words that do not need an -s to make them plural. There are no rules to help you with irregular plurals, but most of them are very common words, for example:

man → men   person → people

Activity 1

Write down the irregular plural for the following words. Use a dictionary if you need help, and learn the spellings.

foot   child   tooth   ox

Foreign words

See Unit 1, page 15 on the origin of words

Some words that have been taken into English from other languages often keep the plural form of the original language. These plurals have to be learned and remembered.

Activity 2

Use a dictionary to find the meaning and the plural of each word below. Learn how to spell them, too!

1 oasis   2 cactus   3 larva
4 phenomenon   5 stimulus   6 criterion

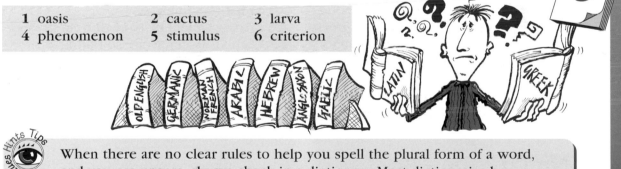

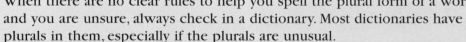

When there are no clear rules to help you spell the plural form of a word, and you are unsure, always check in a dictionary. Most dictionaries have plurals in them, especially if the plurals are unusual.

Activity 3

Write out the sentences below, changing the words in blue into plurals. They are all foreign words, irregular plurals or no change plurals. Use a dictionary if you need help.

1 Look at those flying goose!
2 How many trout did you catch?
3 Lots of man, woman and child hate mouse.
4 Head louse prefer to live in clean hair.
5 Today has been packed with different crisis!

Plurals: self-tests

Complete the tests below. When you have finished, your teacher will have the answers to check against.

Self-test 1

Write down the plural form of the words in blue.

1 Skateboard can be dangerous.
2 Cigarette give you lung cancer.
3 That's two football you've burst.
4 We pay too many tax.
5 Macbeth met three witch.
6 Your joke are awful.
7 Look at those lightning flash.
8 The wicket-keeper took six catch.
9 Dinosaur had tiny brains.
10 There are more boss than workers.

Self-test 2

Write down the plural form of the words in blue.

1 Not all cars have radio.
2 I want two go on the roller-coaster.
3 An orchestra has many cello.
4 What are all those stereo worth?
5 Buffalo have huge, curved horns.
6 Fire torpedo!
7 Many houses have patio nowadays.
8 Dingo will eat almost anything.
9 Very few Eskimo live in igloos.
10 Rodeo are very popular in America.

Self-test 3

Write down the plural form of the words in blue.

1 How many midwife do you know?
2 Do all Porsches have sunroof?
3 A cat has nine life.
4 Road tariff are a good idea.
5 Giraffe must suffer with sore throats!
6 A good card player can spot bluff.
7 A good alarm will deter thief.
8 Different tribes had different chief.
9 Did all the dwarf fancy Snow White?
10 Sheaf are gathered at harvest time.

Self-test 4

Write down the plural form of the words in blue.

1 Motorway cost a fortune to build.
2 I like westerns where cowboy lose!
3 The two army faced each other.
4 I hate writing essay.
5 Lorry should be banned from towns.
6 School assembly are so boring.
7 All of the puppy survived.
8 Three goals, all from volley.
9 Local community can be very strange.
10 That field is full of pony.

Self-test 5

Write down the plural form of the words in blue.

1 Lots of person think hunting for deer is cruel and should be stopped.
2 All the postman went on strike when they had to deliver unwrapped cactus.
3 There are three series about aircraft on TV at the moment.
4 Child should brush their tooth regularly but often hate doing it.
5 Caged mouse need many varied stimulus to stop them from getting too bored.

WELL DONE for the answers that you got right! If you got any wrong, go back to the part of the unit that will help you. Work through the activities again until you get them right.

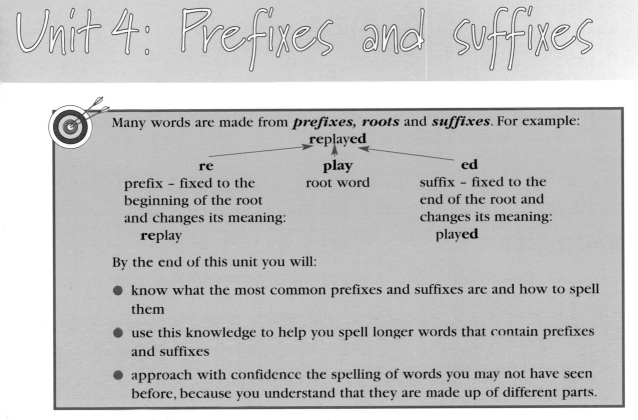

Many words are made from **prefixes, roots** and **suffixes**. For example:

replayed

re	**play**	**ed**
prefix – fixed to the beginning of the root and changes its meaning:	root word	suffix – fixed to the end of the root and changes its meaning:
replay		play**ed**

By the end of this unit you will:

● know what the most common prefixes and suffixes are and how to spell them

● use this knowledge to help you spell longer words that contain prefixes and suffixes

● approach with confidence the spelling of words you may not have seen before, because you understand that they are made up of different parts.

Prefixes

Rule

A prefix is a group of letters that are fixed to the **front** of a root word and change its meaning. In most cases neither the root word nor the prefix changes its spelling when they are fixed together. For example:

view   **inter**view   **pre**view   **re**view   **over**view

root   prefix

Activity 1

The main prefixes that you will use are shown below. Use the rule above to match up each prefix with a root word. Write the new words, and label the prefix and the root. The first one has been done for you.

un	agree	**pre**	dress
dis	growth	**anti**	climax
under	build	**over**	behave
im	fasten	**mis**	view
re	possible		

Prefixes

Do not worry if the last letter of the prefix 'doubles up' with the first letter of the root when you follow the rule. Remember, neither the prefix nor the root changes when you fix them together:

dis + solve = di**ss**olve   un + necessary = u**nn**ecessary

Activity 2

Write down as many words as you can by matching up the prefixes and roots below.

Prefixes		Roots		
dis	mis	rated	natural	spent
un	under	spell	react	satisfied
over	il	similar	moral	logical
im	in	numerate	rule	

Activity 3

Read what the student below has written about her spelling. She has made the top ten spelling mistakes when using prefixes! Can you spot the misspelt words? Write out the correct spelling of the words and use a dictionary to check them.

WSS Wickton Secondary School
Pupil report: English   Name: Sue McNally

The teacher says that my spelling is quite good. It is allways a dissappointment when I get allmost every word right but still make unecessary misstakes with prefixes. I must stop mispelling words like ilegal and imature and learn the main rule: neither the root word nor the prefix changes its spelling when they are added together. The teacher says that allthough it may seem unatural, it's something that must be targeted.

Prefixes

Activity 4

The sentences below tell you about Sam's bungee jump. The words in blue have a missing prefix. Choose the correct prefix for each word from the following list and write out the new word.

anti	dis	im	in	over
pre	under	un	re	mis

1. Sam felt __pleasant.
2. He had ___judged how frightened he would be.
3. _____neath him the buildings looked like matchboxes.
4. He was __capable of leaping off this crane.
5. Why had he agreed to this __possible bungee jump anyway?
6. Imagine the ___comfort of being three hundred feet up in the air with only a rubber rope stopping you from hitting the ground!
7. The security girl __moved his safety chain.
8. He was _____come with fear.
9. But if he backed out now it would be such an ___climax.
10. He asked the girl if every last ___caution had been taken. She smiled and shoved him off the crane. Five seconds later he was hanging upside down with a massive smile on his face. He'd done it!

Suffixes

Rule

A suffix is a group of letters that is fixed to the **end** of a root word and change its meaning. For example:

deliver   deliver**y**   deliver**ance**   deliver**ed**   deliver**s**

root   suffix

When a root word ends in a **consonant**, in many cases neither the root word nor the suffix changes its spelling when they are fixed together. For example:

rest   rest**ing**   rest**ful**

Activity 1

The roots and suffixes below have been taken from a review of a dance event at a summer festival. Match each root to the correct suffix, and write out the new word.

sound	**ness**	mix	**ship**
colour	**ing**	friend	**est**
cool	**ful**	bright	**ed**

Activity 2

Use your imagination to write a review of the dance event. Include the words you have written out in Activity 1. You could start your review like this:

DJ Judge Cool is the **brightest** star in the dance universe …

Suffixes: adding -ful to roots

> **Rule**
>
> When the suffix **-ful** is added to a root word, it only needs one **l**.
> For example:
>
> hope**ful** not hope**full**

Activity 1

Can you find the seven hidden **-ful** words in this grid? Write them in your spelling notebook.

L	U	F	E	C	A	E	P
R	L	U	F	E	P	O	H
P	O	W	E	R	F	U	L
L	U	F	E	N	U	T	T
O	L	X	S	R	F	I	C
G	R	A	T	E	F	U	L
L	U	F	T	S	A	O	B
C	H	E	E	R	F	U	L

Activity 2

Read the postcard below. The writer has not remembered the rule about adding the suffix **-ful** to a root. Write the postcard out properly.

Dear Gran,
Weather dreadfull, food disgracefull. We'll be thankfull when the two weeks are up. Glad you're not here to share this awfull, hatefull experience.

Lots of love, Andy

Granny Smith
Apple Cottage
Fruitford
Cl DER

Activity 3

Use the word bank below to write a postcard telling a friend how good a holiday has been. Remember to be care**ful** with the **l**!

hopeful	delightful	boastful
cheerful	plateful	grateful
powerful	tuneful	peaceful

Suffixes and roots: when to keep 'e'

Rule

When you add a suffix starting with a *consonant*, such as **-ful**, **-ment**, or **-less** to a root ending in **e**, you usually keep the **e** then add the suffix. For example:

root	consonant suffix		new word
hope	+ ful	=	hop**e**ful
price	+ less	=	pric**e**less
amuse	+ ment	=	amus**e**ment
excite	+ ment	=	excit**e**ment

Activity 1

Match each root below with the correct *consonant suffix* and write down the new word. The first one has been done for you.

disgrace	**ment**	blame	**ment**
care	**ness**	hope	**ness**
disagree	**ful**	like	**ful**
false	**less**	excite	**less**

1 If a root ends in a soft **ce** or **ge**, the **e** is usually kept when the suffixes **-able** or **-ous** are added. For example:

noticeable, courageous

2 When a root ends in **e** and is added to a suffix that starts with a vowel (for example, **-able**, **-ing**, **-age**), a few words can be spelled with or without an **e** like the examples below:

root + suffix	with an 'e'	without an 'e'
like + able	likeable	likable
love + able	loveable	lovable
age + ing	ageing	aging

Activity 2

Match each stem below with the correct *vowel* suffix. Write out the new words. The first one has been done for you.

notice	**able**	outrage	**able**
knowledge	**ous**	peace	**ous**
courage	**able**	manage	**ous**
change	**able**	advantage	**able**

Suffixes and roots: when to drop 'e'

Rule When you add a suffix starting with a *vowel*, such as **-able**, **-ed**, **-ing** (*vowel* **suffix**) to a root ending in **e**, you usually drop the **e** before adding the suffix:

root	vowel suffix	new word	root	vowel suffix	new word
amuse + ing	=	amusing	cure + able	=	curable
forgive + ing	=	forgiving	excite + ed	=	excited

Activity 3

Match each root word below to a *vowel suffix*. Remember to drop the **e** from the root when you add it.

place ⟶ **es**	believe	**er**
forgive **ation**	educate	**ed**
invite **en**	force	**ing**
excite **able**	desire	**able**

Activity 4

All the *roots* in the table below end in **e**. The *suffixes* start with either a vowel or a consonant. Copy out and complete the table by adding each root to the suffix and writing out the new word. Use the rules you have learned to decide whether to keep the **e** on the root.

Root	+	Suffix	New Word
force	+	ful	**forceful**
ache	+	ing	**aching**
believe	+	ed	
service	+	able	
clue	+	less	
advertise	+	ment	
move	+	able	
forgive	+	ness	
admire	+	ing	
adore	+	able	
desire	+	ed	
home	+	less	
amaze	+	ment	
age	+	less	
care	+	less	
argue	+	able	
agree	+	ment	
defence	+	less	
recharge	+	able	
create	+	ing	

Suffixes and roots: doubling

Rule

When you add a suffix that starts with a *vowel* (-**ed**, -**er**, -**ing**) to a root that ends in a *consonant*, you usually need to double the last letter of the root. For example:

chop + ed = cho**pp**ed   chop + ing = cho**pp**ing
chop + er = cho**pp**er   chop + y   = cho**pp**y ('y' as a vowel sound 'e')

This rule only applies to words that have:

● ONE *syllable*: (**chop**)
● ONE short vowel: ch**o**p
● ONE consonant: cho**p**.

This is known as the ONE, ONE, ONE rule.

Activity 1

Try the ONE, ONE, ONE rule on the words below. Take the rule step by step.

Step 1
Write out the words from the list below that have **one syllable**.

wet	forest	dog	beauty	pie
steal	spoon	pet	ape	slob
pit	sag	dim	pat	red
gut	step	root	grab	bid
caravan	quit	change	answer	stab
team	bat	steep	thirst	sea
treat	net	see		

Step 2

Read through your list of one-syllable words. Underline words with **one short vowel** sound. For example: p**i**t but not p**ie**.

Step 3

Look at the words you have underlined. Tick the words that have **one consonant after the vowel**. For example: sta**b** but not se**e**.

For more help on short vowel sounds see Unit 2, page 25

44

Suffixes and roots: doubling

Activity 2

You should now have a list of seventeen words which fit the ONE, ONE, ONE rule. Choose seven of these words and match them to as many of the vowel suffixes below as you can. (Note: not all of the suffixes will go with all the words.) Write out the new words. Remember to double the final consonant of the root word.

| -er | -ish | -ing | -en | -ed |

Activity 3

Copy out and complete the warning sign below. Add the missing suffixes in the box below to the words in blue. Remember to use the doubling rule.

| -ing | -y | -ers |

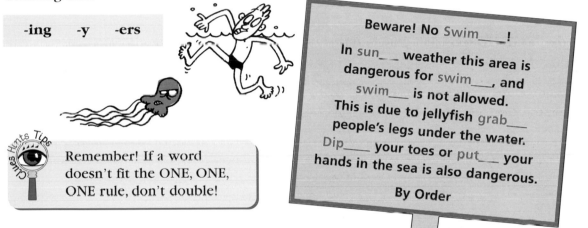

Remember! If a word doesn't fit the ONE, ONE, ONE rule, don't double!

Beware! No Swim____!

In sun__ weather this area is dangerous for swim____, and swim____ is not allowed. This is due to jellyfish grab____ people's legs under the water. Dip____ your toes or put___ your hands in the sea is also dangerous.

By Order

Activity 4

Each word in blue in the sentences below needs a suffix. Choose which suffix to add from the following box, and write out the new word. Use the ONE, ONE, ONE rule to work out where you need to double.

| -ing | -ed | -ish |

1 I've decided, I'm finally quit___ eating chocolate.
2 After all, I'll soon be hit___ 15 years old!
3 I know I'll be gut___ every time I walk past a sweet shop!
4 But one thing's for sure. I won't be step___ inside.
5 I don't want to end up with a sag___ stomach, do I?
6 I'll never be a slob___ couch potato again!
7 No more steal___ chunks from you.
8 I won't be grab___ anyone else's chocolate either!
9 I've done so well I deserve pat___ on the back.
10 Oh, go on then! As it's an offer not to be repeat___, I'll have a little bit!

45

Suffixes and roots: the 'l' rule

Rule

If you add a suffix that starts with a vowel (-ed, -ing) to a root word that ends with an **l**:

- if the **l** follows a single vowel it is doubled, for example:
  cancel → cance**lled**   travel → trave**lling**

- if the **l** follows a pair of vowels it is never doubled, for example:
  appeal → appea**led**   conceal → concea**ling**

- if the **l** follows a vowel and an **r** it is never doubled:
  hurl → hur**led**   curl → cur**ling**

Activity 1

Students often make mistakes with the words below. Copy and complete the table. Follow the **l** rule.

Stem ending in 'l'	Add 'l'	Add vowel suffix	New word
cancel	l	ing	
cancel	l	ation	
rebel	l	ing	
control	l	ing	
travel	l	ed	
travel	l	er	
instal	l	ation	
spiral	l	ing	
label	l	ed	
model	l	ing	
marvel	l	ous	

Activity 2

Read the advice label below. Choose which vowel suffix from those in the box to add to each word in blue. Use the **l** rule. Write out the new words.

-ing
-ed
-ous

Label___ According to Government Regulations
ADVICE – BEFORE INSTAL____ THIS GAME!
Yes! I know how much you grovel__ to your mum and dad to make them buy you this, and that playing this computer game will be fulfil___ your wildest dreams. But wait and all will be reveal__

In five minutes time you'll be travel___ through the cosmos at warp 8, propel___ by four Stealth megaton engines. You'll be quarrel___ with your brother or sister about who's going to play and channel____ your energy into this incredible action-packed, marvel___ masterpiece.

THE ADVICE?   FASTEN YOUR SEATBELT!

Suffixes and roots: changing 'y' to 'i'

Rule

When adding a suffix to words that end in **y**:

● if there is a **vowel** before the **y**, you just add the suffix. For example:

enj**o**y → enjoyed   pr**a**y → praying   pl**a**y → playful

● if there is a **consonant** before the **y**, change **y** to **i**, then add the suffix. For example:

co**p**y → cop**ied**   re**pl**y → repl**ied**   inj**ur**y → injur**ies**

Activity 1

Read the following report. Choose a vowel suffix from the box below to add to each blue word, using the rules above. Write out the new words.

-ies
-iest
-ed
-ied
-ly

The lady and gentlemen of the jury heard that the man had committed several burglary and had only been caught after being hurt. Sam Swag's injury were caused when he'd been carrying the heavy widescreen television out of a shop during a robbery. He had been painfully delay after dropping it on his foot. When asked why he'd done it, he reply uneasy, 'I wanted to see if I'd be on *Crimewatch* this week.'

Exception! If you add the suffix **-ing** to a word ending in **y**, whether it has a vowel or consonant before the **y**, always just add **-ing**. For example:

carry → carry**ing**;   hurry → hurry**ing**

Activity 2

Read the following extract. Choose a vowel suffix from the box below to add to each blue word, using the rules above. Write out the new words.

-ies   -ing   -ied   -iest   -ed

Admiral Nelson had lots of victory and destroy many ships belonging to his enemy. He went to sea at the age of 12, and had lots of injury during his life, including losing his eye in 1794 and his arm in 1797. His mighty conquest came at the Battle of Trafalgar where, terrify the opposition, he carry his navy to success in 1805. Unfortunately he never enjoy his triumph because he died in this battle. The French navy suffered the heavy losses. His quality and ability remain mystery. History books will never stop portray him as the greatest admiral ever.

Prefixes and suffixes: self-tests

Complete the tests below. When you have finished, your teacher will have the answers to check against. If you got any wrong, go back to the part of the unit that will help you. Work through the activities again until you get them right.

Prefixes: self-test 1
In each sentence, write down the correct spelling in blue.

1 I'm afraid I disagree / dissagree with tests.
2 The pupils always missbehave / misbehave in art lessons.
3 That new player is underated / underrated, in my opinion.
4 The tennis umpire overruled / overuled the line judge.
5 She allways / always makes a fuss of him.
6 The referee sent him off after inumerable / innumerable fouls.
7 That goal should have been dissallowed / disallowed.
8 Those boys are so imature / immature.
9 The dinner is almost / allmost ready.
10 That roller coaster was very unerving / unnerving.

Suffixes: self-test 2
Make two lists from the words below of:
a) suffixes that start with a vowel
b) suffixes that start with a consonant.

11 enjoyment
12 eating
13 beautiful
14 soften
15 blameless
16 fasten
17 foolish
18 washable
19 happiness
20 craftsmanship

Suffixes: self-test 3
Add a suffix to each word in blue below, so that each sentence makes sense. Write out the new word.

21 This friend____ has lasted 40 years.
22 That is an outrage_____ hat!
23 What a comfort_____ sofa!
24 That football__ is a brilliant player!
25 The dark_____ in that attic frightens me.
26 Music is very relax____.
27 He annoys me – he's so boast__!
28 The local paper report__ the match.
29 The dentist said it wouldn't be pain____.
30 Well done, you did brilliant__!

Self-test 4: Suffixes and roots: 'y' to 'i' rule
Add a suffix to each word in blue below, so that each sentence makes sense. Write out the new word.

31 I find adverts very annoy____.
32 She's the brainy_____ girl in the class.
33 I used to be rich but now I'm penny____.
34 'Sorry, Mr Leach, I'm delay__ because I slept in this morning.'
35 I'm well known for my clumsy____.
36 Captain Flint was looking for bury____ treasure.
37 Bully____ is still a problem in most schools.
38 That comedian is the funny____ I've ever seen.
39 Isn't that just the most beauty_____ sports car you've ever seen?
40 Lots of improvements are being carry____ out at my school.

Prefixes and suffixes: self-tests

Self-test 5: Suffixes and roots: 'e' rule

Add a suffix to each word in blue below, so that each sentence makes
sense. Write out the new word.

41 What are the arrange_____ for the wedding?
42 That is totally unforgive____!
43 Use sun block on your nose to prevent sore____.
44 The *X-Files* is brilliant but it's so unbelieve____!
45 Grandad is close to retire____ age.
46 I forgot my key so I force__ the back door open.
47 The policeman was close__ watching the house across the street.
48 Ph6 Cream delays the age___ process.
49 'Thank you very much,' said the girl polite__.
50 If there's one thing I can't stand, it's late____!

Self-test 6: Suffixes and roots: 'l' rule

Choose the correct spelling of the words in blue below. Write
down the correctly spelled word.

51 I think that supermarket labelling / labeling should be clearer.
52 The school bully, Andrew Brown, was expeled / expelled for fighting.
53 I hate peelling / peeling potatoes.
54 Swampy was a New Age Traveler / Traveller.
55 The pilot was controlling / controling the plane.
56 Building the Channel Tunnel involved tunneling / tunnelling for 25 miles.
57 It is essential to prevent signaling / signalling failures.
58 Dogs are marvellous / marvelous companions.
59 The water in the bath was boiling / boilling hot.
60 The Gunpowder Plot was a rebelion / rebellion against royalty.

Self-test 7: Suffixes and roots: doubling

Choose the correct spelling of the words in blue below. Write
down the correctly spelled word.

61 Manchester is weter / wetter than most cities.
62 This hill is steeper / steepper than that one.
63 Scratch off panel to reveal hiden / hidden prize.
64 We've just had a new kitchen fitted / fited.
65 I've got to learn stopping / stoping distances to pass my driving test.
66 I'm tired out! I've been runing / running around all day.
67 I feel I've been treated / treatted badly.
68 Our lights at home have got dimmer / dimer switches.
69 That man is a joger / jogger. He's really fit.
70 The weather in Greece was very suny / sunny.

Many words have common letter patterns and spelling rules that go with them. By the end of this unit you will be able to:

● know the difference between **soft** and **hard** letter sounds and use the rules that go with them

● know when to use **ci** or **cy**

● spell words properly that have **ph** in them

● use the **i** before **e** rule

● understand when to use **ch**, **sh** or **tch**

● choose when to use **ou** or **ow** in a word

● select the right **w** letter pattern

● spell **q** words accurately.

Soft and hard letters

The letters **c** and **g** have different sounds in different words.

The letter **c** has a hard sound in these words:

cry **c**amel a**c**tion musi**c** **c**omputer **c**ustard

The letter **c** has a soft sound in these words:

fa**c**e **c**ity **c**ylinder **c**ell sau**c**e **c**igar

The letter **g** has a hard sound in these words:

graffiti **g**un ar**g**ue ba**g** **g**lory **g**oal

The letter **g** has a soft sound in these words:

gym **g**enius dama**g**e sur**g**eon **g**entle **g**iraffe

Activity 1

Write down a sentence that includes both hard and soft **c** letter sounds and hard and soft **g** letter sounds.

Soft 'c' spellings

- The letter **c** usually has a soft sound when it is followed by **e**, **i**, or **y**, for example:

  city   **cy**linder   sau**c**e

- The letter **c** has a hard sound when it is followed by **a**, **o**, **u**, or a **consonant**:

  cat   **c**ot   **c**ut   **cr**ack.

Activity 1

Sort the following words into those that have soft and hard **c** sounds. Write them out under the correct heading.

carpet	fancy	excited	copper	crow	scanner	celery
decent	centre	captain	precise	clever	cymbal	

Activity 2

Some people get confused about where they should spell a word with **s** and where they should use a soft **c**. Read the pairs of words below and write down the word that is spelled correctly. Use a dictionary if you need help.

1 centigrade / sentigrade   *2* place / plase   *3* mictake / mistake
4 race / rasc   *5* worce / worse   *6* centimental / sentimental
7 cituation / situation   *8* univerce / universe   *9* paradise / paradice

Activity 3

It is easy to confuse words ending with **ice** and **iss**. Read these words:

bliss	hiss	hospice	justice	poultice	Swiss

Count the number of *syllables* in each of the words listed above.

1 How many syllables do the words ending in **iss** have?
2 How many syllables do the words ending in **ice** have?

Rule   Words that rhyme with -**iss** and have more than one syllable are usually spelled -**ice**. **Exception**: lettuce!

Activity 4

Words that are spelled with an -**ace** ending can sound very similar to -**iss**/-**ice** endings.
The following words end with -**ace**. Write a sentence using each word.

furn___	neckl___	pal___	surf___	terr___

Soft 'cy' and 'ci' spellings

When c is followed by **y** or **i** it makes a soft sound. For example:

cycle   spi**cy**   **ci**rcle   ran**ci**d

When you hear a word that ends with a soft sound **cy**, how do you know when to use **cy** (as in fan**cy**) or **sy** (as in gip**sy**)?

There are not many rules to help with this, but more words are spelled with the **cy** ending, such as: Tra**cy**, agen**cy**. If you are unsure, check in a dictionary.

Activity 1

Write down the correct spelling for any words the student got wrong in this test.

1. truansea	2. gipsy	3. racing	4. embassy	5. bouncy
6. cignal	7. citizen	8. plasid	9. infansee	10. civil
11. lunasy	12. fluency	13. cygnet	14. sircle	15. fussy

Activity 2

The words in blue in this newspaper story all contain soft c spellings.
Complete each word correctly using **ice**, **ace**, **ce**, **ci** or **cy**.

Top Star in Priva__ Scandal

There were s__nes of violen__ when i__ skating a__ Kiera Manson discovered *Goodbye* magazine had printed sau__ pictures of her on their __ntre pages. She stormed into the company offi__s and threw chairs around the pla__. The star intends to sue for invasion of priva__.

'These people are a men___,' she fumed. 'How can I live a __vilised life when __rtain photographers for__ me into secre__? They are all prejud___d against me; I'm __rtain they'll __rculate more pictures. They haven't an oun__ of de__n__ in them.'

Goodbye staff had better take not___: the last photographer Miss Manson spotted around her residen__ required an ambulan__!

The letter **c** is the consonant that has the largest number of different sounds. It can sound like:

k in cat	**q** in cute	**s** in city
sh in ocean	**ch** in cello	**ks** in access

It can also be silent: s**c**issors.

Soft 'g' spellings

- The letter **g** usually has a soft sound (sounds like **j**) when it is followed by **e**, **i**, or **y**. For example: ag**e**, **g**in, **g**ym

- The letter **g** usually has a hard sound when it is followed by **a**, **o**, **u**, or a consonant. For example: **g**ain, **g**oat, **g**un, **g**row

There are quite a few common words where **g** followed by **i** or **e** has a hard sound. Write these words in your spelling notebook:
get   geese   gear   tiger   gift   girl   give   begin.

Activity 1

Sort the following words into those with soft and hard **g** sounds. Write them out under the correct heading.

great   ginger   danger   dungeon   dagger   energy
game   garlic   gymnastics   gunfight   gang   ghost
glamour   bug   magic   goal   cage   giant   gem   green

As a very rough guide:
The words with a soft **g** sound spelled with **j** often have the vowels **a**, **o**, or **u** following the **j**. For example,

jacket,   **j**olly,   **j**ust

The words with a soft **g** sound spelled with **g** often have the vowels **e**, **i**, or **y** following the **g**. For example,

trag**e**dy,   trag**i**c,   g**y**mnast

Activity 2

Read the advertisements below. Write out and complete the words in blue with the correct spelling for the soft **g** sound.

Man or mouse?

Aller_ic to exercise? Hate eating ve_etables? Hate _ogging? _udo make you ill? Anything ener_etic a turn-off?

Then _oin the _entleman's _ymnasium, a _entler approach to staying healthy.

_ournalist **wanted!**

Must have experience of _apan, _ermany, _amaica and _ordan. May visit dan_erous places and contact secret a_ents.

Under _eneral control of _eneva HQ. Intelli_ent people ur_ently needed.
Closing date _une 10.

'-ge' and '-dge' endings

No English word ends with a **j**. **-ge** or **-dge** is used instead.

● If there is a *consonant* before the soft **g** sound, add -ge: la**rge**, ra**nge**

● When there is a *vowel* before the soft **g** sound:
  - if the word is **one syllable** and the vowel is a **short vowel**, the word usually ends in **-dge**: ba**dge**, e**dge**, bri**dge**, do**dge**, fu**dge**
  - otherwise, the word usually ends in **-ge**: pa**ge**, messa**ge**, gara**ge**, colle**ge**, hu**ge**

Activity 1

Make a table like the one below. Sort out the words in the box into types of soft **g** endings. Write them down under the correct heading.

hosta__	tru__	posta__	refu__	gru__	ba__	char__
fri__	obli__	voya__	e__	sausa__	banda__	ple__
lozen__	chan__	reven__	ju__	bri__	colle__	

Consonants before soft g: add -ge	Short vowel before soft g, one syllable: add -dge	Other words with soft g sound: add -ge

Activity 2

The following headlines have some mistakes in the soft **g** words. How many can you find? Write the headlines correctly.

CARNAGE AS REBELS BESIEGE VILLADGE!

TEENAGE SYRINDGE SCARE!

VINTADGE CAR PRICES PLUNGE!

WORKERS ALLEGE PORRIGE STORAGE SAFETY SCANDAL!

STRANGE ALIEN MESSADGE FOUND IN VILLAGE!

TAX DODGE WILL DAMADGE PENSION PACKAGE

PRIME MINISTER TO ARRANGE SAFE PASSADGE

OUTRAGE AT BELOW AVERIDGE RESULTS

SALVADGE MEN WON'T BUDGE

SERIOUS DAMADGE IN SEWADGE SLUDGE LEAKAGE

Activity 3

Invent five headlines for your local newspaper. Each one must have at least two **-ge** or **-dge** endings in it.

'ph' words

The **f** sound in a word is usually spelled with **f** or **ff**, but is sometimes spelled with **ph**:

focus   coffee   **ph**one
life   cuff   gra**ph**

Most of the words using the **ph** pattern came from the Ancient Greek language. Remember that knowing the origin of words can help you to remember the different spelling patterns.

physics   **ph**enomenon
or**ph**an   **ph**armacy   **ph**ilosophy

Turn back to Unit 1 page 15 for more information about the history of words.

Activity 1

Write down the answers to these quiz questions. Every answer is a word containing the **ph** letter pattern.

1 Starts with A, finishes with Z, has 26 letters.   a _ _ _ _ _ t
2 Another word for a ghost.   _ _ _ ntom
3 Huge animal with big ears and a trunk.   e _ _ _ _ _ _ _
4 A book about someone's life.   b _ _ g _ _ _ _ y
5 Musical instrument.   xylo _ _ _ _ _
6 When a big star signs their name for you.   auto _ _ _ _ _
7 School subject, humanities.   ge _ _ _ _ _ _ y
8 School subject, science.   _ _ y _ _cs
9 Not my niece, but my …   ne _ _ _ w
10 The punctuation mark in the word *don't*.   apo _ _ ro _ _ _

Activity 2

The student below made some mistakes with words that use the **ph** letter pattern. Write out correctly any words that she has got wrong. Use a dictionary if you need help.

1 Albert Einstein was a fisicist.
2 Roald Dahl wrote *Phantastic Mr Fox.*
3 One of the best orchestras is the London Symphony Orchestra.
4 Measles and tyfoid are bad illnesses.
5 *The Daily Telegraff* is a leading broadsheet newspaper.
6 Phertiliser and compost are good for the garden.
7 Egypt is famous for the Pyramids and the Sphinx.
8 Remember to use full stops, commas and paragraffs correctly.

55

'ei' or 'ie' spellings?

Rule The following rule is useful to remember:

i before **e** except after **c** but only when the **ie** sound rhymes with 'me'.

- **i** *before* **e** and rhymes with **me**, for example: bel**ie**ve, f**ie**ld
- **i** *after* **e** because it doesn't rhyme with **me**, for example: **ei**ght, h**ei**ght
- **i** *after* **e** when after **c**, for example: rec**ei**ve, c**ei**ling

Watch out for the **exceptions** to this rule!
Use Look, Say, Cover, Write, Check to learn them:

seize   protein   weird   caffeine   neither   counterfeit   weir   either
science   ancient   And the names: Keith   Neil   Sheila

Activity 1

Read the newspaper article below. Complete the words in blue correctly
with either **ie** or **ei**. Write out the correct words.

BANK BES__GED!

A br__f s__ge took place at Midwest Bank this morning, at __ght o'clock.

A cash__r sounded the alarm when a man attempted to dec__ve her into bel__ving that he was using his own cheque book. The th__f panicked and produced a gun. An armed police team entered the building. There was a f__rce gun battle and loud shr__king. Onlookers felt at the h__ght of their anxiety. But to everyone's rel__f, no one was hurt.

Police Ch__f Williams said afterwards, 'As soon as I rec__ved the word to go, he'd had it. I don't know what the f__nd thought he could ach__ve.'

Activity 2

Correct this student's spelling test. Write out correctly any word that she
has spelled wrongly. Check in a dictionary if you need help.

1. yield	2. concieve	3. handkercheif	4. greivous	5. sheild
6. perceive	7. niece	8. reciept	9. retrieve	10. wield
11. preist	12. piercing	13. ceiling	14. peice	

'ei' or 'ie' spellings?

See Unit 4 page 47 for the rule on suffixes changing from y to i

● When adding a *suffix* to a word ending in **y**, always use **ie**, even after a **c**. For example:

fancy → fanc**ie**d   emergency → emergenc**ie**s

cie words:

● when spelling a word where **cie** sounds like **sh**, the **i** comes before the **e**. For example:

an**cie**nt   spe**cie**s   defi**cie**nt   suffi**cie**nt   cons**cie**nce

Two separate sounds:

● if you can hear that an **i** and an **e** make two separate sounds in a word, spell the word as you hear it and ignore other rules. For example:

science (sc**i** / **e**nce)   society (so / c**i** / **e**t / y)
audience (au / d**i** / **e**nce)   convenient (con / v**e** / n**i** / **e**nt)

'ei' words

Remember:

● when the **ie** sound rhymes with **me**, it is usually spelled with **ie**, for example:

sh**ie**ld   f**ie**ld

● When the **ie** sound doesn't rhyme with **me**, it is usually spelled with **ei**, for example:

for**ei**gn   forf**ei**t   th**ei**r   w**ei**ght

Activity 3

Say each of the words below to yourself and listen for a long **ee** sound.
Write out correctly any word that has been spelled wrongly.

height   rien   heiress   grieve   mischeif
vein   veil   freight   siesmic   pierce

Activity 4

Write a short police report based on the newspaper article in Activity 1 on page 56. Make sure you include words with the **ei** and **ie** letter patterns.

Muddleton Police Station: Incident Report Form

Incident date: _____   Reported by (Officer No.): _____

I was called to Midwest Bank this morning at eight o'clock …

'sh', 'ch' and 'tch' words

The sounds made by the letter patterns **sh** and **ch**, and **tch** and **ch** can sound alike. For example:

| **sh**ip | bro**ch**ure | swi**tch** | **ch**ains |

'tch' and 'ch' words

As a very rough guide!
Words are often spelled with the **tch** letter pattern if the **ch** sound follows immediately after a *short vowel* sound.

| sw**i**tch | h**u**tch | sk**e**tching | p**a**tch | wr**e**tched |

See Unit 2, page 25 for help with short vowel sounds

Exceptions! ch follows a *short vowel* sound in the following words:

atta**ch**   ba**ch**elor   deta**ch**   du**ch**ess   mu**ch**
ri**ch**   sandwi**ch**   su**ch**   tou**ch**   whi**ch**

Activity 1

Read the postcard below. The words in blue need **ch** or **tch** to complete them. Write out the correct words. Use a dictionary if you need help.

Dear __arlie,

This place is brilliant. The __aps here can tea__ us a thing or two about having fun. Sun is scor__ing, bea__ is fantastic, in easy rea__ of the hotel and you don't spend hours sear__ing for somewhere to have lun__. Met a great Du__ girl but don't worry – not getting hi__ed just yet! Been fishing but didn't ca__ anything, just wa__ed the girls on the ben__ next to me!! Back next week – even managed to get the Big Ma__ on the TV – heaven!!

See you soon,   Mick

__arlie Foster
Poa__er's Cottage,
Sco__ Lane,
Mar__ington,
Man__ester,
England

Activity 2

Invent four sentences that have the following words in them:
Sentence 1: change, match, rich
Sentence 2: challenge, crutch, which
Sentence 3: chicken, match, much
Sentence 4: choke, switch, touch.

'ch' or 'sh' and 'ch' or 'k'?

'ch' or 'sh' words

See Unit 1 page 15 for the history of word

Many of the words where **ch** sounds like **sh** came into the English language from French. For example: bro**ch**ure, **ch**andelier, **ch**arade, **Ch**arlotte.

Activity 1

Some people get confused about where they should spell a word with **sh** and where they should use **ch**. Read the pairs of words below and write down the word that is spelled correctly.

1 champagne / shampagne	*2* champoo / shampoo
3 chadow / shadow	*4* chiffon / shiffon
5 machine / mashine	*6* cheriff / sheriff
7 achamed / ashamed	*8* chovel / shovel
9 chauffeur / shauffeur	*10* flaching / flashing

'ch' or 'k' words?

In some words the letter pattern **ch** has a **k** sound. Most of these words came into the English language from Greek. For example: anar**ch**y, **ch**emist, e**ch**o, me**ch**anic, monar**ch**.

As there is no rule about when to use **ch** for the sound **k**, you just have to learn the words! Write them in your spelling book.

Activity 2

Read the product wrappers below. Can you spot six spelling mistakes? Write out the words correctly.

Charter's
chrysanthemum seeds

Anckor
best margarine

best
Schotch whisky

Christmas chards

SALGON X
relief for painful
stomack ackes

Relieve your cronic
back problems with
Johnson's Heat Cream

Activity 3

Decide which of the words below is spelled correctly. Write out the correctly spelled words.

1 orchestra / orcestra / orkestra	*2* bachon / bacon / bakon
3 panich / panick / panic	*4* character / caracter / karacter
5 charaoke / caraoke / karaoke	*6* scheme / sceme / skeme
7 technology / tecnology / teknology	*8* chronicle / cronicle / kronicle
9 architect / arcitect / arkitect	*10* rechless / recless / reckless

'ou' letter patterns

The **ou** letter pattern can make many different sounds:

ow as in m**ou**se   **u** as in tr**ou**ble

or as in y**ou**r   **er** as in fav**our**   **our** as in dev**our**

Rule

When spelling words with the sound **ou/ow**:

ow is used:
- before **n** or **l** when it is the *last* letter of a **root** word such as: fr**ow**n, pr**ow**l, g**ow**n, **ow**l.
- at the end of a word *or* the end of a syllable such as: h**ow**, s**ow** (female pig), sh**ow**er, v**ow**el.

ou is used:
- for most other words with the sound **ow**: spr**ou**t, c**ou**nt, cl**ou**d

Watch out for **exceptions** such as **crowd, foul** and **noun**.

Activity 1

The words below need **ow** or **ou** to complete them. Write out the words correctly using the rules above. Use a dictionary if you need help.

1 n__	*2* m__ntain	*3* t__el	*4* p__er	*5* gr__nd
6 sh__ting	*7* p__nd	*8* sc__t	*9* fl__t	*10* f__nd
11 r__ (argue)	*12* ab__t	*13* ar__nd	*14* c__er	*15* __nce

Activity 2

The short vowel sound **u** can be spelled using **u** as in c**u**p, and **ou** as in c**ou**rage. There are no clear rules to follow. If you are unsure about spelling these kinds of words, note them in your spelling book and learn them.

Write down the correct word from each pair below.

1 encourage/encurage	*2* trouble/truble	*3* soung/sung
4 enugh/enough	*5* couple/cuple	*6* young/yung

It is usually when **r** is added to the **ou** pattern that the rest of the **ou** sounds in the box at the top of the page are made:

or (rhyming with *floor*), such as: y**our** c**our**t f**our**
our (rhyming with *power*), such as: dev**our** s**our** h**our**
er (rhyming with *her*), such as: fav**our** col**our** rum**our**

A small number of **ou** words sound like **oo**, for example: c**ou**pon r**ou**te s**ou**p y**ou**th

'w' letter patterns

Rule

The letter **w** often changes the sound of a vowel that follows it.
For example:

was   **wa**r   **wo**rm

When **w** is followed by **a** it sounds like **o** (as in shot): w**a**s wh**a**t w**a**nt

Watch out for **water** and words that end with silent **e** such as **wave**.

S

Activity 1

Write down the words with **w** letter patterns shown in these pictures.
Use a dictionary if you need help.

Rule

When w is followed by **ar**, it sounds like **or** (as in for). w**a**rble w**a**rden w**a**r

Activity 2

The answers to the clues below all use the **w** letter patterns. Write down the
answers, using the correct spelling. Use a dictionary if you need help.

1 A room in a hospital.
2 A cupboard to keep clothes in.
3 Snow White knew seven of them.
4 Word used when bees fly from a hive: a _____ of bees.
5 When countries fight.
6 Not too cold, not too hot: a moderate temperature.

Rule

When **w** is followed by **or**, it sounds like **er** (as in h**er**): w**o**rm w**o**rd w**o**rse

Watch out for **worn**, **sword**, **worry** and words that end with silent **e** such as **woke**.

S

Activity 3

Choose between **er** and **or** to complete the **w** letter patterns in the
words below. Write down the correct spelling. Use a dictionary if you
need help.

Mist_ _   w_ _ k   j_ _ k   w _ _ th   w_ _ ship

'q' letter patterns

Rule In English, the letter **q** is always followed by the letter **u**. These two letters are then followed by another *vowel*: qu**a**lity, qu**e**stion, qu**i**z

Activity 1

In a **qua** letter pattern, **qu** sounds like **kw** and **a** sounds like **o** (as in h**o**t):

quarantine   squa**b**ble

sounds like: **kw o**   **kw o**

The following words have been spelled as they sound. Write down each word with the correct spelling.

skwod   kwolity   skwot   skwolid   kwolify   skwonder

Activity 2

For more on the history of words, see Unit 1, page 15

When the letter pattern - **que** appears at the end of words it makes a **k** sound. Most words with this pattern came into English from French. Complete the following words adding -**que**. Write down each completed word. Check in a dictionary for the meaning of any word you do not know, and write down what it means.

mas___   cli___   brus___   opa___   obli___

Activity 3

The answers to the questions below all use **que** or **qua** letter patterns. Write down the answers, using the correct spelling. Use a dictionary if you need help.

1 Cash one in a bank.   ch_____
2 A place to dig for rock.   _____ry
3 An indoor sport; a drink.   _____sh
4 A Muslim place of worship.   mo_____
5 The only one of its kind.   un_____
6 An argument.   _____el

The **que** letter pattern can be spelled **ck** in American spelling: cheque → check

Always use English spelling in your writing.

See Unit 8, page 97 on Americanisms.

Common letter patterns: self-tests

Complete the tests below. When you have finished, your teacher will have the answers to check against.

Self-test 1: soft 'c'
Write down the words in blue that are spelled correctly.

1 The surface / surfase of the cylinder / silinder was a centimetre / sentimetre wide.
2 The cinnamon / sinnamon was specially cent / sent from a certain / sertain shop.
3 Cider / sider tastes rancid / ransid if left to cettle / settle for too long.
4 It is a cerious / serious error for cyclists / syclists to ride in cement / sement.
5 The circumference / sircumference of the cigar / sigar was mascive / massive.
6 A cecret / secret legacy / legasy lay in the cellar / sellar.
7 The cell / sell had poor cecurity / security so escaping was a cinch / sinch.
8 He was placid / plasid, centimental / sentimental and very celfish / selfish.
9 We must cease / seace this lunacy / lunasy of selling off the cemetery / semetary.
10 Not a cingle / single illicit / illisit cilicon / silicon chip was found.

Self-test 2: soft 'c'
Write down the words in blue that are spelled correctly.

1 Were you miced / missed at the office / offiss party?
2 Why the grimace / grimiss on your face? Is something amice/amiss?
3 I noticed / notissed that you enjoyed the practice / practiss.
4 Don't simply dismice / dismiss him as a menace / meniss.
5 After the service / serviss the car's engine was still hicing / hissing.

Self-test 3: soft 'g'
Write down the words in blue that are spelled correctly.

1 A gentleman / jentleman does not generally / jenerally ask a lady's age / ajc.
2 If that is a genuine / jenuine gewel / jewel I'm very gealous / jealous.
3 My gerbil / jerbil ate some gelly / jelly and ginger / jinger.
4 The gelignite / jelignite caused a gigantic / jigantic explosion on the get / jet.
5 I'm a ginx / jinx. I'll geopardise / jeopardise the geography / jeography trip.
6 People from any generation / jeneration or gender / jender can have the gob / job.
7 The giraffe's / jiraffe's legs went spongy / sponjy after drinking the gin / jin.
8 The clergy / clerjy geered / jeered at the burning effigy / effijy.
9 Gigging / Jigging up and down generated / jenerated a gingling / jingling sound.
10 Don't gest / jest. We're eating genetically / jenetically modified oranges / oranjes.

Self-test 4: '-ge' or '-dge' endings
Write down the words in blue that are spelled correctly.

1 What do you need to rummage / rummadge in that hege / hedge for?
2 Get the oil because this hinge / hindge won't budge / buge.
3 He's got the edge / ege. I've lost the advantadge / advantage.
4 Did you manadge / manage to win? Your knowlege / knowledge is amazing.
5 I hope the lodger / loger got my messadge / message.

Common letter patterns: Self-tests

Self-test 5: 'ph'
Write down the words in blue that are spelled correctly.

1 The last phase / fase of the conpherence / conference was a triumph / triumf.
2 The pheasant / feasant was phinally / finally shot emphatically / emfatically.
3 The man from the pharmacy / farmacy is a phencing / fencing phanatic / fanatic.
4 I must emphasise / emfasise that there is a hole in our atmosphere / atmosfere.
5 Pay phones / fones are a phraction / fraction of the cost of mobiles.
6 That prophet / profet has the belieph / belief that he can see the phuture / future.
7 The biography / biografy I've just phinished / finished was phantastic / fantastic.
8 I'm phascinated / fascinated to know which paragraph / paragraff is best.
9 The graph / graff shows the catastrophe / castatrofee this season has been.
10 Am I phantasising / fantasising or are you claustrophobic / claustrofobic?

Self-test 6: 'ei' or 'ie'?
Some of the words in blue in this advert are spelled wrongly. Write down
the correct spelling for each word.

It is unbeleivable when you discover how many people ignore their personal hygeine.
You don't have to be concieted to be efficient and keep your body clean. You must
just beleive that you are going to try the patience of your friends and cause their
nostrils a lot of greif if you don't! If you have aggreived friends we can help to bring
some releif. As experts in our field, we have turned washing into a sceince. Others
have tried to copy us, but if you really want to retreive your friendships, don't decieve
yourself. Wiegh up the consequences if you don't call us now. You'll receive our
special 'Emergencies only' pack within 24 hours. Seize the opportunity and call
us now!

Self-test 7: sh, ch and tch
Write down the words that
are spelled correctly.

1 pich/pitch
2 ostrich/ostritch
3 couch/coutch
4 lach/latch
5 sachel/satchel
6 purchase/purtchase
7 skech/sketch
8 strecher/stretcher
9 march/martch
10 sandwich/sandwitch

Self-test 8: sh, ch and tch
Write down the words that
are spelled correctly.

1 speech/speetch
2 scrach/scratch
3 thacher/thatcher
4 unstich/unstitch
5 wreched/wretched
6 kichen/kitchen
7 torch/tortch
8 crouch/croutch
9 quench/quentch
10 bucher/butcher

Self-test 9: sh, ch and c/k
Write down the words that
are spelled correctly.

1 chaos/kaos
2 school/skool
3 moustache/moustashe
4 loch/lok
5 chef/shef
6 charate/karate
7 parachute/parashute
8 chovel/shovel
9 chemistry/cemistry
10 echoes/ecoes

Common letter patterns: self-tests

Self-test 10: 'ou'/'ow'
Write down the words spelled correctly.

1 down/doun
2 spowted/spouted
3 pownce/pounce
4 drowning/drouning
5 bownce/bounce
6 fowntain/fountain
7 nown/noun
8 crown/croun
9 howling/houling
10 owtside/outside

Self-test 11: 'ou'
Write down the words spelled correctly.

1 cusin/cousin
2 dunce/dounce
3 dubble/double
4 bught/bought
5 cupple/couple
6 hunting/hounting
7 cunntry/country
8 nurishment/nourishment
9 cutting/coutting
10 yunger/younger

Self-test 12: 'w' letter patterns
Use **a** or **o** to complete each word in blue. Write down the word.

1 Be careful not to w_nder off and fall into the sw_mp.
2 That w_tercolour painting looks all wr_ng.
3 I w_nder if that is a 100 w_tt light bulb or a 60 w_tt.
4 I wish I could w_ve a magic w_nd and have a w_d of cash.
5 I w_nt to exercise to get rid of my w_bbly belly!
6 Wh_t sort of w_rranty did you get with that car?
7 When the w_lf stared at him he sw_llowed nervously.
8 She w_ddled like a duck but didn't w_nt to change.
9 The new w_shing machine w_s completely useless.
10 W_tch out for those w_ffles – they taste really awful.

Self-test 13: 'w' letter patterns
Write down the words in blue that have been spelled correctly.

1 A warlock / worlock is another name for a wizard.
2 After all that effort I'm warn / worn out.
3 Open the window, it's too worm / warm in here.
4 I've got a wart / wort right on the end of my nose.
5 Look out! Here comes the traffic worden / warden.

Self-test 14: 'q' letter patterns
The words in blue have been spelled as they sound. Write down the
correct spelling for each word.

1 Sorry, you're not kwolified to run this skwodron.
2 The earthkwake ruined all my anteeks so kwickly.
3 To answer that kwestion you need to figure out the right kwontity.
4 I rekwire a new pump for my akwarium.
5 That kwaint cottage looks so picturesk, it's not skwolid at all.
6 My skware kwilt needs washing after I spilled likwid on it.
7 People freakwently get skwoshed on the underground in London.
8 The kween did very badly in the pub kwiz.
9 May I enkwire why you kwodrupled my bill?
10 Two kworters eekwal a half.

Unit 6: Common endings

Many word endings follow common letter patterns.
This unit will help you to:

● improve your spelling of common letter patterns at the end of words
● improve your spelling of endings that sound the same but are spelled differently.

'-ough' endings

The letter pattern ending -**ough** has many different sounds.

Activity 1

The following words all end in -**ough**, but are said in different ways. Copy out the table below. Put the words underneath in the correct column, according to how they sound.

rhymes with:	puff	toe	off	cow
	rough	though	cough	plough

although   bough (branch of tree)   dough   tough   enough   trough

Activity 2

Write a passage with the title: Tough Stuff! Include at least one of each type of word ending in -**ough** from your table above.

'-ought' and '-aught' endings

The letter patterns ending -**ought** and –**aught** can each be said in different ways.

Activity 3

Copy and complete the following table of -**ought** and -**aught** letter patterns. Put the words underneath the table in the correct column.

rhymes with sport		rhymes with craft
-ought	-aught	-aught
brought	caught	draught

bought   daughter   laughter   naughty   nought   ought   onslaught   thought

Activity 4

Draw a 10cm square grid. Design a word search that includes as many of the -**ough**, -**ought** and -**aught** words on this page as possible.

'-ous', '-ious' and '-eous' endings

The **uss** sound at the end of many words can be spelled in three ways: -**ous**, -**ious** and -**eous**. Listen carefully to the word you are trying to spell, and you should be able to choose the correct ending.

'-ous' endings

> **Rule**
>
> The ending -**ous** is the most common letter pattern at the end of an **adjective** or describing word, for example:
>
> | noun | | adjective |
> |---|---|---|
> | poison | → | poison**ous** |
> | danger | → | danger**ous** |

Activity 1

Read the advertisement below. Write out the words that have the -**ous** ending and underline the -**ous** end pattern.

Don't be nervous!
Come inside now and experience the world famous

- MUSEUM OF STRANGE AND FABULOUS THINGS -

✦ Poisonous tarantula spiders
✦ Dangerous three-eyed toads
✦ Monstrous colour-changing chameleons
✦ Measure yourself against the height of the most enormous man who ever lived!

Your friends will be jealous when you tell them you've been. Don't miss these marvellous sights.

Come inside NOW!

Activity 2

Design an advertisement for a theme park attraction of your choice. Use as many -**ous** words as you can.

'-ious' and '-eous' endings

> **Rule**
>
> The ending **-ious** is mainly used in two cases:
> 1 When you hear the sound **shus** at the end of a word, following the letters **t, c** or **x** as in: ambi**t**ious deli**c**ious an**x**ious
> 2 When you can hear the **i** as a syllable on its own, for example:
> curious   furious   mysterious
> cur / **i** / ous   fur / **i** / ous   myster / **i** / ous

Activity 1

Read this encyclopaedia entry. List the words that end in **-ious**.

> **The Great Pyramid:** Built 4500 years ago at Giza in Egypt, this monument is probably the most mysterious and precious man-made structure on the planet. How the ingenious people of the time managed to construct a perfectly formed pyramid made from about 6 million tons of rock remains unknown. The curious Pharaohs' tombs were believed to contain curses and infectious diseases, designed to stop ambitious and devious robbers stealing their contents.

Activity 2

Copy and complete this table. Use words from your list from Activity 1.

'shus' sound following 't', 'c' or 'x'	'i' as a syllable heard on its own
mysterious	ingenious

See Unit 5 page 50: Soft and hard letters

> **Rule**
>
> Use the **-eous** ending when:
> - a root ends in soft **-ge** as in: advanta**ge** → advanta**geous**
> - you can hear an **e** in a word as a syllable on its own as in: hid**e**ous.

Activity 3

Copy out and complete the following table. Put the words underneath into the right column. Use joined writing, so the action of writing **e** and **o** together will help you remember the letter pattern.

'-eous' on roots ending in soft -ge sound	'e' as a separate syllable sound
Advantageous	Hideous

courteous   courageous   piteous   gorgeous   simultaneous
outrageous   spontaneous   miscellaneous

'-tion', '-ssion', '-cian' and '-sion' endings

The -**shun** sound at the end of some words can be spelled in the following ways:

-**tion**	emotion	-**cian**	magician
-**ssion**	confession	-**sion**	television

There are rules that will help you decide which ending to use. They help you to listen to a word carefully and make the right choice.

'-tion' endings

> **Rule**
> - Use the ending -**tion** if you can hear a *long vowel* before the **shun** sound, for example: st**a**tion, compl**e**tion, p**o**tion, revol**u**tion
> - Use the ending -**tion** if there is a *consonant* before the **shun** sound: instru**c**tion, fra**c**tion
> - Use the ending -**tion** after a *short vowel* **i** sound when the word doesn't end in **mission**: exhib**i**tion, cond**i**tion

See Unit 2 page 24: Vowels and consonants

Activity 1

Read the advertisement below. Write down the words ending in -**tion**.

VENTURA INDOOR KARTING

Attention all speed freaks! Forget relaxation, and experience incredible action!

- Karts in tip-top condition with incredible acceleration
- Prizes for high speed course completion
- A truly unbeatable sensation!

PLUS: THIS MONTH'S PROMOTION!
Deadly Destruction Derby
STOCK CAR PILE UP EXHIBITION – the ultimate exhilaration

TELEPHONE 01145 2456778

Activity 2

Underline the letter just before the -**shun** sound in each word that you wrote down in Activity 1. Make a table like the one below. Now sort out your words into the three types and put them in the correct columns.

Long vowel before shun sound	Consonant before shun sound	After short vowel i sound (doesn't end in -mission)
relaxation	action	exhibition

'-ssion' endings

'-ssion' endings

> **Rule**
>
> - Use the ending **-ssion** if you can hear the *short vowel* sounds **a**, **e** or **u**, before the **shun** sound:
>
>   comp**a**ssion, poss**e**ssion, disc**u**ssion
>
> - Use the ending **-ssion** after the *short vowel* sound **i** when the word ends with **-mission**. Otherwise use **-ition**:
>
> | short 'i' ending '-mission' | short 'i' not ending '-mission' |
> |---|---|
> | em**i**ssion | exhib**i**tion |
> | adm**i**ssion | add**i**tion |

Activity 1

Read the following play script. Write out the words that have the **-ssion** letter pattern at the end, and underline the short vowel which comes before it.

CARETAKER:	The admission charge is £2.50 and that's final.
BOY :	I'm not paying that.
CARETAKER:	Then you don't have permission to go in there.
BOY :	Yes I do. It's my school disco.
CARETAKER:	*(with smug expression)* I'm not having a discussion about it, laddie.
BOY :	*(with aggression)* Have some compassion! I've got no cash!
CARETAKER:	Don't look at me with that expression. You're NOT getting in!
BOY:	Wait till I tell my dad about this. We'll both be back!

Remember! If you hear the sound **-mission** at the end, use **-ission**. Otherwise use **-ition**.

Activity 2

Read the after-match commentary below. The words in blue need to be completed using the ending **-ssion** or **-tion**. Write down the correct words.

The team had never played against more difficult opposi____ and as the sad proce_____ of losing players left the pitch their ambi____ must have been in tatters. In the discu____ at half time, the captain apparently said it wasn't their fault. The competi_____ was far better. The only consola____ for his team was that the condi____ were bad. Thankfully the players decided that they weren't going to be beaten into submi___ and went out after half time with a great deal of enthusiasm and pa_____. The score at the end was 3-3.

'-cian' and '-sion' endings

'-cian' endings

Rule The ending -**cian** is used when a word refers to a person's job or occupation: magician, optician, mathematician, beautician.

Activity 1

Write down four other jobs with the -**cian** ending.

'-sion' endings

Rule You can usually hear words that end with -**sion** as they have a slightly different sound. For example:

-**zhun** as in televi**sion**   *instead of*   -**shun** as in admi**ssion**

Exceptions! Watch out for: apprehension, mansion, tension, comprehension.

Activity 2

Write down the words in blue below, using the -**sion** ending.

1 What's your ve_____ of the story?
2 The two cars crashed in a terrible coll_____.
3 My glasses really improve my v_____.
4 Floods! Follow the dive_____ signs.
5 My birthday was a brilliant occ_____.
6 I'm going to watch te_____ tonight.
7 That ref's dec_____ was rubbish!

Activity 3

Read the advertisement below. The words in blue need to be completed with one of the following endings: -**tion**, -**cian**, -**ssion** or –**sion**. Write down the correct words. Use a dictionary if you need help.

Anthony Gell School – The School With Vi_____.

NOW OFFERING GCSE IN CARTOONS/ANIMA____!
Finally students have permi_____ to make films and draw cartoons in the classroom! Want to study how cartoons get from the drawing board to the televi____? This course shows you! Create the ac____ yourself. From explo____ to slow mo____ sequences, you make all the deci____. Create your own vi____ and become a techni____ of the art of cartoon expre_____. Why not accept this mi_____? One more thing ... There's no examina____, so no revi____! GCSE anima____ is 100% coursework. Act on your enthusiasm and pa_____! Sign up now!

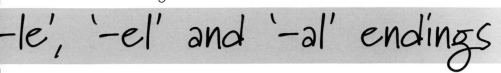

'-le', '-el' and '-al' endings

The endings **-le**, **-el** and **-al** are used when you can hear an **-ul** sound at the end of a word. For example:

castle   barrel   animal

'-le' endings

Most words ending in the **-ul** sound are spelled with **-le**, such as ap**ple**. There are no clear spelling rules for this ending, but the activities below will help you get them right.

Activity 1

Draw a 12cm square grid with each box measuring 1cm x 1cm and design a word search that includes the words below. The challenge is to include all of the words!

apple	battle	ankle	baffle
sizzle	angle	beetle	cycle
bottle	candle	circle	bundle
cuddle	chuckle	dazzle	handle

'-el' endings

Rule

The **-el** ending is commonly used after the following letters: **n**: chan**nel**
r: bar**rel**   **s**: wea**sel**   **v**: re**vel**   **w**: to**wel**   **soft c**: par**cel**   **soft g**: an**gel**

Activity 2

Make a table like the one below. Put the words underneath in the correct column according to which letter comes before the **-el**. The first one is done for you.

after 'n'	after 'r'	after 's'	after 'v'	after 'w'	soft 'c' or 'g'
channel					

channel   flannel   jewel   panel   barrel   quarrel   trowel   vessel
tassel   level   angel   kennel   travel   shovel   tunnel   towel   vowel

Activity 3

Make up a **_mnemonic_** (see Unit 1, page 10) to help you remember the letters which an **-el** ending follows.

N	R	S	V	W	C	G

'-al' endings

● -al is often used as an ending for an *adjective* (describing word). For example:

an accident**al** crash

Here, the -**al** makes the word mean 'to do with'. In other words, to do with an accident.

● A few words ending in -**al** are nouns or naming words. There is no rule to tell you whether to use -**al**. For example:

anim**al**	arriv**al**	cryst**al**	funer**al**
med**al**	ped**al**	riv**al**	sign**al**

Activity 1

Read the extract below which shows a number of words with the -**al** ending. Write out the words and underline the -**al** ending.

A MAGICAL MANUAL OF CLAIRVOYANCE*
by
Mystical Madam Marge

*Clairvoyance: Noun meaning power of seeing things not present to senses, second sight.

Activity 2

Using your imagination, think of a book and write a contents page for it that uses some adjectives with the ending -**al**. Use the word bank below to help you.

abnormal	colossal	educational	fatal
accidental	confidential	electrical	geographical
ancestral	dental	emotional	herbal
archaeological	cosmological	environmental	historical
artificial	critical	equal	hysterical
astrological	diabolical	eternal	identical
classical	digital	experimental	international

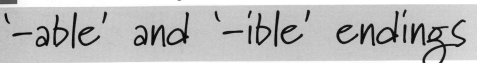

'-able' and '-ible' endings

There is no clear rule to help you choose when to use the ending **-able** (as in cap**able**) or **-ible** (as in ed**ible**). But there are two things that might help you:

1 More words end in **-able** than **-ible**.

2 You can sometimes hear whether the ending is **-able** or **-ible**, for example:

sens**ible** or break**able**

'-ible' endings

Activity 1

All the answers to the quiz below end in **-ible**. Write down the answers and learn them. Get someone to test you!

1 wise and reasonable = se_s___
2 awful and creepy = ho_r___
3 amazing and extraordinary = in_red___
4 dreadful and ghastly = t_rr___
5 reachable and handy = ac_e_s___
6 unseen = in__s___
7 fairly likely = po_s___

Activity 2

All the missing words in the following extract end in **-ible**. Write down the correct words. Your answers in Activity 1 will give you extra clues!

Poisonous Mushrooms

1. The red and white mushrooms are *inedible.*
2. Eating them will make you feel _____.
3. It would be _____ to buy a guide book.
4. They are very _____ with pictures and descriptions.
5. They will stop you making a _____ mistake.
6. It may sound _____ but it is _____ to die from eating poisonous mushrooms.

'-able' endings

Activity 3

Design a colourful poster advertising ZEST – a new soft drink. Use the wording below in your advert, ending each word in blue with **-able**.

This new drink is prefer____ to other predict____ drinks on the market. Its tangy fruit flavours will turn you from a boring depend____ Billy 'No Mates' to a fashion___ and notice____ super cool dude. The other brands are all avoid____ when you've got ZEST inside you. It's the remark___ choice, for the remark____ individual.

'-ical', '-icle' and '-acle' endings

The endings **ical** (as in mag**ical**), -**icle** (as in ic**icle**) and -**acle** (as in tent**acle**) sound similar, but have different purposes. Words ending in -**ical** are much more common than the other two endings.

'-ical' endings

The -**ical** pattern is often used at the end of an adjective or describing word (see page 73). Further examples of the -**ical** ending are:

| ident**ical** | med**ical** | phys**ical** | techn**ical** |

Activity 1

Many -**ical** adjectives are used in your school subjects. Make a table like the one below. Complete the words ending in -**ical**. They are arranged in the subject areas you would find them in.

The Arts	The Sciences	The Humanities	Technology
alphabet____	m__ical	hist____	t___nical
_nalytical	log___l	geo_____	mech__ical
lyri___	_iological	_hysi_al	elec_____
metaphor___	_ptical	bibl____	
mus___	pr___ical		

'-ical' '-icle' and '-acle' endings

'-icle' and '-acle' endings

Words ending in -**icle** and -**acle** are nouns or naming words, and they are not very common. They include:

art**icle**	obst**acle**
chron**icle**	part**icle**
ic**icle**	spect**acle**
man**acle**	tent**acle**
mir**acle**	veh**icle**

Activity 1

Read the newspaper report below. Write out each word that ends in -**acle** or -**icle**, and underline the ending.

The Daily Chronicle

Scientists are baffled and stunned by a new photograph which shows a 30ft tentacle rising out of Loch Ness. The spectacle proves, they say, that the miracle of prehistoric life in the loch may finally prove true. The photograph was taken from a moving vehicle and therefore is a little blurred, but experts say it is unmistakable. Thousands of articles have been written on the subject of 'Nessie'. Previously theories put forward the idea that it might be a distant relative of the dinosaurs. Scientists thought the last obstacle in proving that 'Nessie' didn't exist was removed when a sonar scan of the Loch was made five years ago. The new evidence, however, opens up the debate again.

Continued on page 2

Activity 2

The report in Activity 1 is written in the style of a serious broadsheet newspaper. Use your imagination to design a tabloid newspaper front page for the story about Nessie. Make sure it puts the story across in a more eye-catching and sensational way.

CHALLENGE: Include as many -**icle** and -**acle** words as you can!

'-ance' and '-ence' endings

The word endings -**ance** (as in dist**ance**) and -**ence** (as in sent**ence**) sound very alike. There are no rules to help you decide which ending to use.

Activity 1

Use the word bank below to write down the answers to the clues that follow. Remember to write the correct -**ance** or -**ence** ending for each word!

Words ending in '-ance'	Words ending in '-ence'
import**ance**	sent**ence**
bal**ance**	sil**ence**
perform**ance**	viol**ence**
entr**ance**	evid**ence**
assist**ance**	excell**ence**
appear**ance**	exist**ence**

1 Absolute quietness = _____
2 Used in court to convict criminals = _____
3 Starts with a capital letter, ends with a full stop = _____
4 Doorway into a house = _____
5 An act on stage = _____
6 Being of help = _____
7 Fight or struggle = _____
8 Being alive = _____
9 Two equal weights will = _____
10 Unbeatable quality = _____
11 The way something appears = _____

Activity 2

Find the -**ence** and -**ance** words in this article. List them in two columns according to which ending they have.

A Magical Mystery

The magician's last great performance needed the assistance of the audience. It involved the appearance of a ghostly figure at the side entrance of the theatre. The figure took watches and jewellery from the crowd, who were shocked into silence. No one could explain its existence. The magician's excellence was applauded but at the end of the night there was a mysterious disappearance. The magician had done a runner, leaving only a single diamond ring as evidence. He has never been found.

'-ate' and '-ite' endings

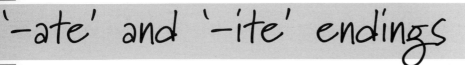

The endings -**ate** (as in termin**ate**) and -**ite** (as in gran**ite**) are usually quite easy to tell apart.

● The ending -**ate** is used most often, and the long vowel sound **a** can be heard very clearly: decor**ate**

● The ending -**ite** usually sounds like a long vowel sound **i**: pol**ite**

● In a few words the ending -ite sounds like a short vowel sound **i**: defin**ite**, oppos**ite**, gran**ite**

Activity 1

Write down the answers to the clues below, using a thesaurus if you need help. Each answer ends in -**ate**. The first letter of each answer will reveal a secret word. Write down what you notice about the letter pattern at the end of this word.

1	To confuse, muddle and make difficult	_ompl_c_te
2	To get rid of. The Daleks did lots of this	_xtermin___
3	Improve and repair an old house	_enov___
4	Change from one language to another	_rans___
5	To copy or behave like someone else	_mit___
6	Very lucky and successful	_ortu__te
7	Instant, done at once	_mm_di_te
8	Often bought as a bar, gorgeous taste	_hoco___
9	A measurement which is a rough guess	_pprox____
10	To finish or cut something short	t__min___
11	To leave the country for good	em__gr__

THE SECRET WORD IS _ _ _ _ _ _ _ _ _ _

Activity 2

Copy out the letter below. Choose the correct word that ends with -ite from the box to fill each space.

quite	favourite	ignite	definite	invite
opposite	write	polite	despite	

Dear Sam

One weekend soon we are going to _ our friends to a barbecue. We can't be _ about the date yet. If it rains, we shall still enjoy ourselves _ the weather, although it is difficult to _ damp charcoal! We shall eat our _ foods – sausages and burgers. To be _, we will have to ask the people in the house _. I'll _ again _soon to give you more details.

See you soon,

Tom

Common endings: Self-tests

Complete the tests below. When you have finished, your teacher will have the answers to check against.

Self-test 1: '-ous', '-ious' and '-eous' endings

Each word in blue below ends in **-ous**, **-ious** or **-eous** and means the same as the word in brackets. Write out each word correctly.

1 env_____   (jealous)
2 advantag_____   (for your good, helpful)
3 outrag____   (shocking or cruel)
4 danger____   (risky)
5 hilar___   (very funny)
6 obliv_____   (unaware)
7 prev_____   (before now, prior to)
8 spontan____   (done without thinking)
9 anonym____   (nameless, unknown)
10 delic_____   (beautiful taste)
11 nox____   (poisonous or dangerous – as in fumes)
12 hid____   (awful, disgusting)
13 feroc_____   (cruel, fierce)
14 obv____   (very clear)

Self-test 2: '-tion' and '-ssion' endings

Each word in blue below ends in **-tion** or **-ssion** and means the same as the word in brackets. Write out each word correctly.

1 introduc____   (at the beginning, start)
2 anima____   (cartoon)
3 confe_____   (admitting something)
4 depre_____   (unhappiness)
5 promo____   (better job)
6 fic____   (made-up story)
7 atten____   (... to detail)
8 emo____   (feelings)
9 discu_____   (friendly talk)
10 concu_____   (bang on the head)

Self-test 3: '-cian' and '-sion' endings

Each word in blue in the sentences below ends in **-cian** or **-sion**. Write out each word correctly.

1 If you want good marks, do more revi____.
2 The magi____ did an incredible trick.
3 Modern computers are made with incredible preci____.
4 The country suffered an inva____ in the year 1066.
5 The politi____ won by 3456 votes.
6 There has been an explo____ of talent in the music industry.
7 Coastal ero____ is a serious problem on the East Coast of England.
8 The electri____ has fixed the cooker.
9 Third divi____ football is exciting to watch.
10 A tacti___ carefully considers which tactics to use.

79

Common endings: Self-tests

Self-test 4: '-le', '-el' and '-al' endings

Each word below ends in -le or -tle.
Write out each word correctly.

1 cand__
2 scribb___
3 cas___
4 cudd__
5 bat___
6 whis__
7 rus__
8 set__
9 sadd__
10 wrest__

Each word below ends in -le or -al.
Write out each word correctly.

1 decim__
2 manu__
3 purp__
4 bott__
5 fin_
6 bubb__
7 surviv__
8 person__
9 dimp__
10 miner__

Self-test 5: '-ical', '-icle' and '-acle' endings

Each word in blue below ends in -ical, -icle or -acle and is the answer to
the clue in brackets. Write out each word correctly.

1 tent____   (part of an octopus)
2 techn____   (to do with the way things work)
3 mir___   (an unbelievable happening)
4 veh____   (a car or van)
5 mag____   (mysterious and wonderful)
6 art____   (found in a newspaper)
7 log____   (clear and reasonable)
8 mechan____   (automatic or done by machines)
9 spect____   (an amazing sight)
10 obst____   (gets in the way of things)

Self-test 6: '-ate' and '-ite' endings

Each word below ends in -ate or -ite.
Write down the word correctly.

1 oppos__
2 irrit__
3 evapor__
4 priv__
5 defin__

Self-test 7: '-ance' and '-ence' endings

Each word below ends in -ance or -ence.
Write down the word correctly.

1 brilli__
2 viol__
3 excell__
4 sent__
5 entr__

WELL DONE for the answers that you got right! If you got any wrong, go
back to the part of the unit that will help you. Work through the activities
again until you get them right.

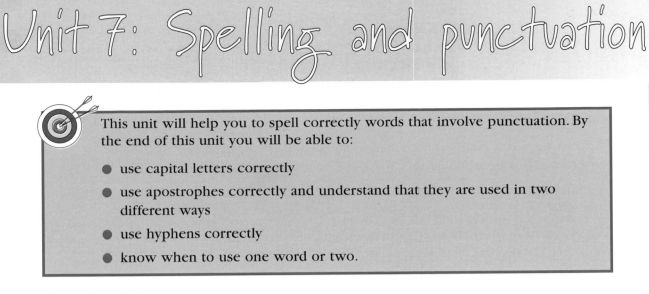

This unit will help you to spell correctly words that involve punctuation. By the end of this unit you will be able to:

- use capital letters correctly
- use apostrophes correctly and understand that they are used in two different ways
- use hyphens correctly
- know when to use one word or two.

Capital letters

The rules for using capital letters are quite simple, but people are often careless when using them!

Rule

Use capital letters for:

- the beginning of a sentence: **T**he striker shot the winning goal.
- all **proper nouns**: **S**cotland, **K**elly, **C**oronation **S**treet
- brand names: **A**didas, **N**ike, **R**eebok
- words that come from proper nouns: **S**cottish, **L**ondoner
- the **pronoun** I or any **abbreviations** involving I: **I**'ve, **I**'m, **I**'ll
- the first word of a speech: Kate said, '**C**an we go home yet?'
- initials: **RSPCA**   **WWF**   **NATO**
- days of the week and months of the year: **M**onday, **J**uly
- the names of specific events: **W**orld **C**up, **B**attle of **B**ritain, **E**aster
- titles: **M**r **M**rs **D**r

Activity 1

When the following sports report was typed, the capital letter key on the keyboard was faulty. Write out the report again, putting in the capital letters.

the football world was stunned today by the resignation of john knee, manager of ditchthorpe rovers. in a brief statement mr knee said, 'it is a sad day for me but i believe that recent results have left me no choice.' club chairman ivor loadercash said, 'it has come as a great shock. the 14-0 home defeat to wigton city on wednesday obviously didn't help, but things will pick up.' a disappointing run has seen ditchthorpe lose 57 games on the trot, during which time they have failed to score a single goal. at a press conference knee said, 'to be honest i'm as sick as a parrot. saturday afternoons will never be the same again.' he then added, 'mind you, i still love the rovers and i'll still be tuning in to the bbc to see how many the lads lost by.'

Capital letters

Activity 2

Write around 100 words about a strong memory that you have, but **do not** put in any capital letters. You must include:

a eight proper nouns   *c* conversation
b initials   *d* the personal pronoun **I**

When you have finished, swap with a friend and correct their work. Swap back and check if all your deliberate mistakes were spotted.

Never use capital letters where they are not needed.
In an examination you will lose marks if you:

- use a capital letter in the middle of a word
- use 'large' letters at the beginning of a word where a capital is not needed.

If your writing includes either of the above, change your style! Claiming 'It's just the way I write' will not help you.

ascender

Size matters. Stop your bad habits now.

Page line

descender

Activity 3

The student's work below has mistakes with capital letters. Write it out again, correcting the mistakes.

when I was very little i went to julie's birthday party. I took her a new nike bag as a present. When Julie openeD it she was really Pleased so I Smiled at her best friEnd katie who had tipped Me oFF about what to buy Her. We played lots of games and then ate Lots of Brilliant food. We aTe Crisps and Cakes and jelly and pop and lots more too. The only proBlem was i started to feel A bit sick. 'what's up with You?' asked tom. i tried to Look normal and replied, 'Nothing, I'm Fine, I've Never Been Better.' i rushed to the bathroom but alex was in there. I daRted into julie's bedroom where all the Presents were stacked. now i'm not saying Where I was sick, but Let's just say that julie's new bag Came in very useful!

Apostrophes

Apostrophes have two uses:

● of abbreviation (for example: do not → don't)
● of possession.

Apostrophes of abbreviation

Rule | The apostrophe of *abbreviation* shows where a letter or letters have been missed out of a word:

do not	I am	they are	let us	we will	it is	we have
↓	↓	↓	↓	↓	↓	↓
don't	I'm	they're	let's	we'll	it's	we've

Activity 1

Read the interview below. Shorten the words in blue by using an apostrophe. Then write them down.

We are delighted, the whole team are. It could not have gone better. Let us face it, we did not expect to make the final at all, it has been a bonus just getting this far. Of course I am delighted to score the winner but it is a team game and we will all be celebrating later on. I would not have scored at all if it had not been for that brilliant pass from Mick. Mick is a terrific player and he is the one who should have all the credit. It has all been brilliant and we have just about deserved it.

Activity 2

Write six sentences about your friends. Each sentence should have one of the following in their abbreviated form in it.

you are	she has	should not	I will	you will	cannot

Clues Hints Tips | It can be very confusing if you miss out an apostrophe when using an abbreviation. For example, if you leave out the apostrophe in **we'll** or **I'll**, you are left with a completely different word and meaning.

Apostrophes

Apostrophes of possession

> **Rule**
>
> An apostrophe of possession shows that something belongs to, or is somehow linked with, something else.
>
> If the 'owning' *noun* is **singular**, add an apostrophe and 's': **'s**
>
> Laura owns a mobile phone → Laura's mobile phone
> There is a pool in the hotel → the hotel's pool
> The idea the scientist gets → the scientist's idea
>
> If the 'owning' *noun* is **plural** (more than one), just add an apostrophe to the 's': **s'**
>
> The teachers have a meeting → the teachers' meeting
> The girls have a changing room → the girls' changing room
>
> ***Irregular plurals*** require an apostrophe and an 's' (like a singular noun) when they are the 'owner': **'s**
>
> The men have a club → the men's club
> The people have a princess → the people's princess

Turn back to Unit 3, page 30, for more help with plurals

Activity 1

Write down how you would you use an apostrophe to show possession between the things in the sentences below.

1 Suzanne owns a yo-yo.
2 The horses have saddles.
3 The joggers have blisters.
4 The television has a remote control.
5 The singer has a manager.
6 The old men have wrinkles.
7 Women have rights.
8 Martin has a dream.
9 Andy makes a choice.
10 The students have a party.
11 The car carries passengers.
12 The cars carry passengers.

Proper nouns that end in 's' can either end with an apostrophe and an 's' or just an apostrophe.

| Robbie William**s's** new CD | *or* | Robbie William**s'** new CD |
| Julia Robert**s's** latest film | *or* | Julia Robert**s'** latest film |

Apostrophes

You must use an apostrophe to show possession even when what is owned does not appear in the sentence.

> I have to go to the chemist**'s** after school.

The apostrophe is still needed because *chemist's* stands for *chemist's shop.* Many shop names should have apostrophes but they often miss them out. *Woolworths* should really be spelled *Woolworth's* as it stands for *Woolworth's shop.* Can you spot any more like this? Make a note of any you come across.

Activity 2

Write the following passage out, selecting the correct word from the choices in blue.

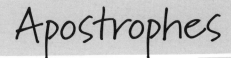

CLAW HAMMER

Its / It's / Its' here at last. This games / game's / games' just awesome, you wont / won't / wont' see anything like it for years / year's / years'. Its / It's / Its' just brilliant. It starts / start's / starts' well and just goes / goe's / goes' on getting better.

(Micks / Mick's / Micks') mega rating: ★★★★★

You are CLAW, the last of the cyber warriors / warrior's / warriors' from Grunyak – friends / friend's / friends' are all dead, planets / planet's / planets' destroyed. Youre / You're / Your the only one whos / who's / whos' left and youre / you're / your after revenge. Claw is angry, hes / he's / hes' furious, he means / mean's / means' business!

Fly to the evil planet Brendok and work through the levels / level's / levels' until you reach the Castle of Anguish. Watch out for the terrifying dogs / dog's / dogs' who guard the entrance. Are you any match for the dogs / dog's / dogs' speed and killer instinct? Use Claws / Claw's / Claws' weapons / weapon's / weapons' to stop them and reach the castles / castle's / castles' power source.

If you cant / can't / cant' buy this game, borrow youre / you're / your mates / mate's / mates' NOW!

Hyphens

> **Rule**
>
> Hyphens are used to join two or more words to make a new word such as:
>
> pre-season training   ready-to-wear football kit
>
> Hyphens can make a big difference to the meaning of a sentence as in:
>
> Football manager: I hope my players will all resign next season.
> Football manager: I hope my players will all re-sign next season.
>
> With some words you can choose whether to use the hyphen or not. For example:
>
> cooperate / co-operate   jet-stream / jet stream

Activity 1

Explain the different meanings created by the hyphens. Write an example that uses each one to show you understand the difference.

1a smelly-school teacher	*1b* smelly school-teacher
2a refuse	*2b* re-fuse
3a record-breaking	*3b* record breaking
4a thirty-odd people	*4b* thirty odd people
5a big home-owners	*5b* big-home owners
6a make-up	*6b* make up

Activity 2

The **prefix** 're' can cause confusion if you do not use hyphens properly with it. Write an example for each word in the box to show that you understand its meaning. Use a dictionary if you need help.

reserve re-serve	restrain re-strain	resort re-sort

When two words joined by a hyphen become very familiar the hyphen is sometimes dropped, for example:

lighthouse multicultural

Hyphens are used to join words that are broken between the end of one line of writing and the start of the next. Do not confuse this way of saving space on a page with the creation of new words and meanings.

How many words?

Be careful not to join two separate words together and write them as one word:

    alot ✘   a lot ✔

Be careful not to separate one word and write it as two words:

    up stairs ✘   upstairs ✔

Each word in the box below is a single word:

| although | underground | upstairs | whereas |

The words in this box are two words:

| a lot | as well | in front | no one |

Activity 1

Choose the correct way to write the words below – one word or two.
Write a sentence using each correct version.

1	infact/in fact	*2*	aswell/as well
3	tomorrow/to morrow	*4*	almost/all most
5	downstairs/down stairs	*6*	inbetween/in between
7	towards/to wards	*8*	motorway/motor way
9	underneath/under neath	*10*	also/all so

Activity 2

Write out the sentence in the box below, correcting any mistakes you find.

Be fore you have ago at getting through amaze, you must be friend a reliable guide.

Mistakes made when deciding whether to use one word or two words are related to the kinds of mistakes made when deciding whether to use a hyphen, or when choosing between *homophones*.

See Unit 8, pages 90–1 for help on homophones.

Spelling and punctuation: self-tests

Complete the tests below. When you have finished, your teacher will have the answers to check against.

Self-test 1: capitals
Write out the following sentences putting in the missing capital letters.

1 a character from a computer game, lara croft, has been used to sell soft drinks.
2 there is a big difference between irish whiskey and scotch whisky.
3 many people think that friday is the best day of the week.
4 the boy crept up quietly behind chris. he silently took his wallet and ran off.
5 is it possible to tell the difference between coke and pepsi?
6 the beatles and elvis presley both had seventeen number one hits in great britain.
7 william williams lived on williams street in williamsburg, kansas.
8 the romans cured toothache by tying toads to their jaws.
9 you have to be sixteen years old to buy cigarettes in the uk.
10 a dog was once arrested in spain for snatching handbags from old ladies.

Self-test 2: capitals
Write out the following sentences putting in the missing capital letters.

1 the only person i care about is myself. do you think i'm selfish?
2 only one team from outside england, cardiff city, has won the fa cup.
3 richard asked, 'if you were born in february, what star sign are you?'
4 'i wish i knew what next week's national lottery numbers were,' moaned philip.
5 a puzzled julie asked, 'does a zebra have black stripes or white ones?'
6 some people say that gcse examinations are getting harder.
7 kate told her mother, 'i'm going to be a pilot and fly for the raf when i'm older.'
8 only six people died in the great fire of london in 1666.
9 if they get very upset, octopuses can actually eat themselves.
10 john turned to sam and said, 'i've had enough of this, let's go to burger king.'

Self-test 3: apostrophes
Make sense of these sentences by putting in the correct apostrophes.

1 Jims CK jacket was a fake.
2 I dont want help from you.
3 Im right, youre wrong.
4 Lets all use Daves pens.
5 The boys toilets were disgusting.
6 My computers a real beauty.
7 The dogs gone crazy.
8 The bikes outside and it wont go.
9 Hummingbirds cant walk.
10 Is this the animals hospital?

Self-test 4: apostrophes
Make sense of these sentences by putting in the correct apostrophes.

1 Ive seen Robin Williams new film.
2 My cars better than Scotts.
3 Ill be in Mr Roberts class next year.
4 The childrens room is over there.
5 Ill fetch Sues things, shes ill.
6 The teams morale was very low.
7 Were next, where were you?
8 Youre right, wed better go.
9 Liverpools form was excellent.
10 Im upset, really I am.

WELL DONE for the answers that you got right! If you got any wrong, go back to the part of the unit that will help you. Work through the activities again until you get them right.

Spelling and punctuation self-tests

Self-test 5: hyphens

Write down the word(s) in blue that are correct.

> 1 Report / Re-port to the Head's office for being so accident prone / accident-prone.
> 2 He's so ill tempered / ill-tempered when he loses at table tennis / table-tennis.
> 3 Don't be so self centred / self-centred if you want to earn respect / re-spect.
> 4 Bear baiting / Bear-baiting is cruel and should be outlawed / out-lawed.
> 5 Some awards presentations / pre-sentations look so cut price / cut-price and tacky.
> 6 Jurassic Park kept prehistoric / pre-historic animals within / with-in its grounds.
> 7 The eagle eyed / eagle-eyed submarine / sub-marine captain stared out to sea.
> 8 The farmhand / farm-hand stood in the farmyard / farm-yard.
> 9 The extraordinary / extra-ordinary match went into extra time / extra-time.
> 10 The murderer's fingerprints / finger-prints were all over the handgun / hand-gun.

Self-test 6: how many words?

Write down the word(s) in blue that are correct.

> 1 I've already/all ready finished washing the tablecloth/table cloth.
> 2 Hamburgers/Ham burgers are a favourite sort of fastfood/fast food.
> 3 The telephone/tele phone is dead. I can't get a dialtone/dial tone.
> 4 I had abit/a bit too much to drink so now I've got a hangover/hang over.
> 5 The fireman/fire man ran straight through the firedoor/fire door
> 6 I'm not infavour/in favour of all this infighting/in fighting.
> 7 I think those school meatballs/meat balls are radioactive/radio active.
> 8 This neighbourhood/neighbour hood gets blamed straightaway/straight away.
> 9 You won't get into that nightclub/night club if you're underage/under age.
> 10 That handbag/hand bag was stolen when you were onduty/on duty, Constable.

Self-test 7: general punctuation

This paragraph covers all the rules in Unit 7. Write it out correctly.

> 'you do fancy her dont you?' screamed shane. 'youve fancied her since that christmas party at janes, havent you?' a crowd was gathering in the corridor, expecting a nother fight. andrew sighed and started to explain again.
>
> 'look shane, this is a big miss understanding. ive told you that this all started last saturday. at her party i told jane that i didnt want to go out with her. she got the hump so made up this story about me and zoe. i dont fancy zoe at all; shes your girlfriend and youre my mate.' shane calmed down abit but he still wasnt sure.
>
> 'thats easy for you to say, but what about the girls netball team? why were they all teasing zoe about you?'
>
> 'no idea. perhaps janes been spreading her lies with them too. look, i swear on my mothers life, i dont fancy zoe and i definitely didnt kiss her at janes party.'
>
> shane smiled and shook andrews hand. 'sorry mate, but i had to find out. no hard feelings?'
>
> 'only if you lend me that new cd youve just bought,' andrew replied with a cheeky smile. shane grinned and nodded his head. friends once more, they went their separate ways. as andrew turned into the dinnerhall, zoe casually walked beside him, and whispered:
>
> 'how about the cinema and a take away from the chinese later?'
>
> 'sure, i'll call for you at seven.'

> This unit will help you to understand some of the more unusual features of spelling. By the end of this unit you will be able to:
>
> ● choose correctly between **homophones**
> ● understand how **silent letters** work
> ● recognise when words are misspelled on purpose
> ● understand that American English uses different spelling rules from standard English.

Homophones

Homophones are words that sound the same but have different spellings and meanings. For example:

> muscle (*strength*) ⟶ mussel (*shellfish*)
> waist (*part of the body*) ⟶ waste (*rubbish*)
> peace (*not war*) ⟶ piece (*of cake*)
> pray (*worship*) ⟶ prey (*hunted animal*)

Clues Hints Tips

Homophones cause problems with computer spell-checkers. A computer spell-checker will only tell you if a word is spelled incorrectly. It will not correct the mistake if you have chosen the wrong word. A computer spell-checker would not find any mistakes in the following passage, for example:

> Bee care full with spell cheques bee cause they own lee sea spelling miss steaks. They are sup posed two save thyme but if ewe do knot luck close lea ewe cud miss sum errors like these.

Activity 1

Explain the difference between the following words. Write a sentence for each word to show you understand its meaning.

1 board / bored   *2* led / lead   *3* meter / metre
4 plain / plane   *5* rap / wrap   *6* right / rite / write
7 site / sight / cite   *8* weather / whether   *9* aloud / allowed

Activity 2

Read the sentences below. Write down each word in blue that is the right one to use so that the sentence makes sense.

1 I accept / except it's my fault but I can't bare / bear it
2 You new / knew that horse would lose / loose the race, didn't you?
3 I here / hear that the special affects / effects in the film are brilliant.
4 The currant / current bet is £100. Do you want to gamble / gambol?

Use a dictionary to find the meaning of the words you DID NOT choose from the sentences above.

Homophones

Activity 3

Eddie has put his work below through a computer spell-checker, but he has not read it carefully. Write it out correctly.

On holly day we stayed in a mass sieve hotel. Even though we were in a busy city our room was very quite as it was on the top floor. Some thymes it gets used as the bridle sweet. Eye new it must have cost a fortune. It was really posh two. Their was a chest of draws sew big that you could sit in it and the hole room had this gold boarder running a round the walls. The food was brilliant as well. The meet was grate and you got lodes of it, especially the stake, and the deserts were delicious to. Even the serials at break fast were lovely. The only bad thing was that it was so posh you had too watch your manors so I wood altar that bit if wee go again.

One knight we sore a scary thunder storm; it really through it down with reign. We all stud on the balcony and lent on the rail to watch it. The lightening was so bright it lit up the sky like a flair gun, I've never scene such a site. It was a pity it past overhead so quickly.

We spent most days on the beech being really idol but that's what holly days are four, isn't it?

Homophones (such as **board/bored**) are one way in which words can be confused, but there are also others.

Homonyms are words that are spelled the same, but have different meanings such as:

> I **saw** the man using a **saw** to cut up the wood.

Homographs (or **heteronyms**) are words that are spelled the same, but are pronounced differently and have different meanings such as:

> Shedding a **tear**, I watched her **tear** up our marriage certificate.

Homophones: 'there', 'their' and 'they're'; 'it's' and 'its'

'there', 'their' and 'they're'

Rule

- **there** has two uses.
  - it shows a place, for example: It was over **there**.
  - it is also used with **verbs**, as in: **There** are seven days in a week.
- **their** means 'belonging to them', for example: It is **their** home.
- **they're** is an **abbreviation** for 'they are'. **They're** mad in that class!

Activity 4

Write out the following extract from a holiday brochure. Fill in the spaces correctly, using **there**, **they're** or **their**.

Once you arrive _____ you'll be amazed by the friendly locals. You'll be invited into _____ homes and invited to share _____ meals. In fact _____ so friendly you won't want to leave. _____ are many beautiful places to visit but try to see the church with its famous windows – _____ rumoured to be at least 300 years old and _____ will be no way to replace them if _____ ever damaged.

If you have problems in using **there**, **they're** and **their**, ask these questions before you choose which one to write:

- Would 'they are' make sense in your writing? If so, choose **they're**.
- Is something being owned by 'them'? If so, choose **their**.
- If neither of the above seems right, choose **there**.

'it's' and 'its'

Rule

- **its** means 'belonging to it', for example: The car has lost **its** wheel.
- **it's** is an *abbreviation* for 'it is' or 'it has': **It's** an easy mistake to make.

Activity 5

The sentences below need to be completed using **its** or **it's**. Write them out, using the correct word.

1. ____ very simple. Remember the dog's muzzle or ____ going to bite us.
2. Because ____ so old the computer has lost ____ usefulness.
3. '____ a lie,' said Joe. '____ a mistake. ____ not me who took the cash.'
4. The engine's dead, ____ losing fuel. ____ fuel pump needs replacing.
5. The android lifted ____ gun. '____ the end for humanity,' it said.

Homophones: 'to', 'too' and 'two'; 'your' and 'you're'

'to', 'too' and 'two'

> **Rule**
>
> - **two** always means the number 2, as in: There were **two** films on TV.
>
> - **to** has two meanings:
>   - it shows the direction 'towards' as in: Let's all go **to** the ark.
>   - it can also be used with a verb to make the **infinitive**, for example: I want **to** run fast.
>
> - **too** has two meanings:
>   - it means 'also' or 'as well', as in: I want to come **too**.
>   - it also means an excess or a surplus (too much), for example: She was **too** noisy.

Activity 6

Write out this conversation. Fill in the gaps with **two**, **to** or **too**.

'Let's go __ the arcade,' said Ian. 'They've got __ brilliant new machines we've got __ try.' He looked over __ his friends.

'I'm not sure. I have __ do that maths before tomorrow. If I go __ the lesson without it I've had it,' replied Andy Ian was not going __ take no for an answer. He looked sharply at John and David.

'Well I hope you __ aren't going __ chicken out,' Ian said.

'Sorry mate, I've got __ do that homework __. I want __ get a decent grade in maths,' replied John. Ian began __ think he was on his own.

'You doing the homework __?' he asked David hopefully.

'Well, I was going __,' David said with hesitation. 'Oh, nuts __ it! It was __ hard anyway! I need __ go out for a bit,' he laughed.

'Brilliant,' Ian said. 'Come on, we'll leave these __ __ do their sad homework.'

'your' and 'you're'

> **Rule**
>
> - **your** means 'belonging to you' as in: Are those **your** trainers?
> - **you're** is an **abbreviation** for 'you are' as in: I'm afraid **you're** wrong.

Activity 7

Write out these sentences. Fill in the gaps with **your** or **you're**.

1 ____ right Kate, ____ new boyfriend is drop-dead gorgeous!
2 Does ____ mum think ____ going to be back for midnight?
3 ____ kidding me. ____ bike isn't half as good as mine.
4 What do you mean, ____ in love with ____ girlfriend!
5 ____ in trouble. Look what ____ dog's done to ____ dad's lawn!

Homophones: 'past' and 'passed'; 'off' and 'of'

'past' and 'passed'

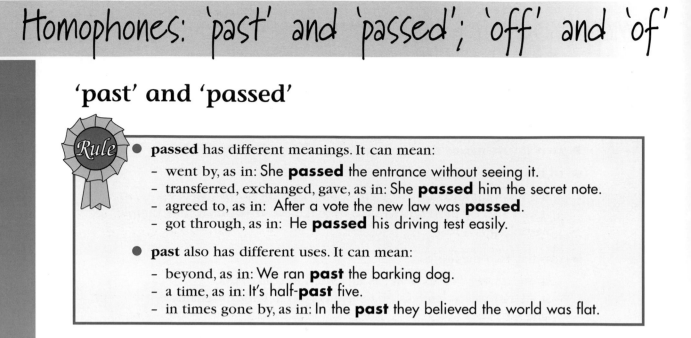

Rule

- **passed** has different meanings. It can mean:
  - went by, as in: She **passed** the entrance without seeing it.
  - transferred, exchanged, gave, as in: She **passed** him the secret note.
  - agreed to, as in: After a vote the new law was **passed**.
  - got through, as in: He **passed** his driving test easily.

- **past** also has different uses. It can mean:
  - beyond, as in: We ran **past** the barking dog.
  - a time, as in: It's half-**past** five.
  - in times gone by, as in: In the **past** they believed the world was flat.

Activity 8

In the rule box above there are four meanings for **passed** and three meanings for **past**. Write a sentence using each meaning of the word correctly.

Activity 9

Write out the sentences below, filling in the gaps correctly with **passed** or **past**.

1 He smiled when he _____ me so I knew he'd _____ his exam.
2 If United had _____ more they'd have got _____ City with no problem.
3 At half-_____ two the council _____ the new rule.
4 We used to argue like crazy but that's all in the _____ now.

'off' and 'of'

Rule

- **off** means the opposite of 'on', for example: He turned the radiator **off**. It can also mean 'away' or 'in motion', as in: He went **off** in a real mood.

- **of** has many meanings. If you don't mean 'away', 'in motion' or the 'opposite of on', use **of**!

Activity 10

Read the following headlines and fill in the gaps correctly with **of** or **off**.

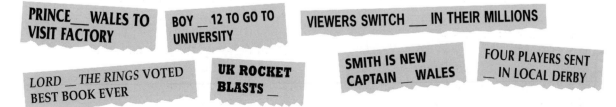

PRINCE__ WALES TO VISIT FACTORY

BOY _ 12 TO GO TO UNIVERSITY

VIEWERS SWITCH ___ IN THEIR MILLIONS

LORD __ THE RINGS VOTED BEST BOOK EVER

UK ROCKET BLASTS _

SMITH IS NEW CAPTAIN __ WALES

FOUR PLAYERS SENT _ IN LOCAL DERBY

Silent letters

Silent letters appear in the spelling of words, but are not heard when the words are spoken aloud:

beret de**b**t **g**naw **h**onest **k**nuckle T**h**omas **wh**ole

> *Clues Hints Tips*
>
> Silent letters make a little more sense if you think about where they come from. In Unit 1, pages 15–17, you learned that English contains many words from other languages. The spelling systems and rules of these languages are all different. For example:
>
> **debt** comes from the Latin word **debitum**
> **knuckle** comes from Old English, when originally the **k** could be heard
> **honest** is from French, a language where the **h** is never pronounced.

Activity 1

Read the problem page from a magazine below. All the silent letters have been missed out of the words in blue. Write the words out correctly.

Dear Aunt Betty
I'm dumstruck. I don't now what to do. Things started to go rong with my girlfriend last autum. I've tried everything - taken her to the balle and the cabare, arranged sutle candle-lit meals, tried to take an intrest in her hobbies. I thought I new her but she won't succum. This has hit me like a bom.
Yours,
Desprately Upset

Dear Desprately Upset
Without a dout you need to get a grip. You'll get diched if you don't start behaving with a little onour. Turn up the temprature and get down on one nee. Without real romance you'll condem yourself to a life of misery searching the personal colums. Sweep her off her feet and remind her how hansome you are.
Yours,
Aunt Betty

Activity 2

Write down the answer to each question below by putting in the missing silent letter.

1 Do it with your ears = lis_en
2 One on each hand = thum_
3 Used on a blackboard = cha_k
4 25th of December = Chris_mas
5 Do it with a pen = _rite
6 Snack food = bisc_it
7 Young cow = ca_f
8 In an art gallery? = ex_ibition
9 Not expecting it = su_prise
10 Sort out money = bu_get
11 Second month = Feb_uary
12 Musical instrument = g_itar
13 Spiky plant = this_le
14 Not obvious = su_tle

Deliberate misspelling

Shops, companies and advertisers often deliberately misspell a word to make it stand out. These misspellings are often a clever play on words that has something to do with the shop or business. For example:

A soft drinks company could use the slogan **Get fizzical**
A hairdresser's shop called itself **Krazy Kuts**
An electrical company might call itself **Sparxx**.

The title of this unit is a deliberate misspelling: 'Misc-spell-aneous'. It contains some of the 'stranger' features of spelling that do not fit easily into the other sections. Why do you think this title has been chosen? (What does **miscellaneous** mean?)

Activity 1

Write down how the deliberate misspellings below should be correctly spelled.

Do not use deliberate misspellings created by advertisers or manufacturers in your own writing. They are misspelling words for a particular purpose – you would just be misspelling them! Learn to recognise these deliberate misspellings when you see them.

Americanisms

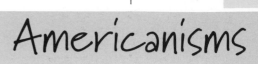

Some American English spellings can be different from Standard English spellings. As people watch American films, buy American products and watch American TV programmes, these spellings are becoming increasingly common.

Activity 1

The words in blue are Americanisms. Write down how they are spelled in Standard English.

The Carlton Hotel
MADISON AVENUE • NEW YORK

We are honored and privileged to welcome you to our hotel. Please refer to this catalog to guide you around all our marvellous facilities.

Our gift center has all your favorite items, ranging from jewelry and cosmetics to evening wear and pajamas. Our entertainers will test your sense of humor and turn a gray day into a bright and colorful one. Our restaurant is the best in town. Try our world famous specialty, the Carlton omelet. We hope you will enjoy your stay.

There are some common differences between American spelling and Standard English spelling. Standard English words ending in **-our** are usually written as **-or** in the US.

Standard English words ending in **-ise** or **-isation** are usually written as **-ize** or **-ization** in the US.

Standard English	→	American English
colour	→	color
recognise	→	recognize

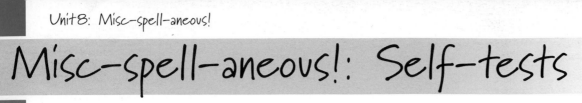

Misc-spell-aneous!: Self-tests

Complete the tests below. When you have finished, your teacher will have the answers to check against.

Self-test 1: homophones
Read each sentence below. Write down the word in blue that is the right one to use so that the sentence makes sense.

1 I'll have to sew / sow up that hole.
2 That's all in the past / passed now.
3 I herd / heard you the first time.
4 Which / Witch one is your bike?
5 You always get you're / your own way.
6 I'll except / accept your excuse today.
7 I hate serials / cereals for breakfast.
8 Smoking is not allowed / aloud.
9 I can't bare / bear this cold wind.
10 There's a draft / draught blowing.

Self-test 2: homophones
Read each sentence below. Write down the word in blue that is the right one to use so that the sentence makes sense.

1 He is a very eminent / imminent man.
2 Do you like currants / currents?
3 Tim's OK, he leant / lent me ten quid.
4 He was my idol / idle years ago.
5 That all seems / seams to be in order.
6 Are you really sure / shore?
7 My tire / tyre has a puncture
8 Have you bean / been to Paris.
9 I challenge you to a duel / dual.
10 Try the new golf course / coarse.

Self-test 3: silent letters
Write out the words in blue with their missing silent letter.

1 The chassi on that car looks broken.
2 Those nats get everywhere.
3 Please nock quietly on the door.
4 Alex Ferguson is a night.
5 Don't drop it, cach it!
6 The climer struggled to the top.
7 I prefer poems that ryme.
8 Who's pinched our garden nome?
9 Can I borrow your hankerchief?
10 I am undoutedly a genius.

Self-test 4: silent letters
Write out the words in blue with their missing silent letter.

1 Are you taking English litrature?
2 It was a very solem ceremony.
3 The dog nashed its teeth.
4 A library is crammed with nowledge.
5 He died from neumonia.
6 Put it in the cuboard.
7 My uncle had a brain haemorrage.
8 Put your nitting down, Mum.
9 How many ours to go?
10 He's the eir to a massive fortune.

Self-test 5: deliberate misspellings
Write down the correct spelling of each word in blue.

1 Don't miss this exclusave offer.
2 R U over 18?
3 Join our Kidz Klub now!
4 Games R Us
5 Klassic Kar magazine
6 Get a little xtra help
7 Easi Flite holidays
8 Summer lovin and summer dreamin
9 Get your eyes tested at See-rite
10 You'll be fizzibly impressed

Self-test 6: Americanisms
Write down the Standard English spelling of each word in blue.

1 What program is on channel 68?
2 My Cadillac needs new tires.
3 Can you take archeology at Harvard?
4 That was a tricky maneuver.
5 That bread has got mold on it.
6 The Redskins have a great defense.
7 He's got a grip like a vise.
8 Is that watch digital or analog?
9 Is that a tin can or aluminum?
10 My Gran tripped over the curb.

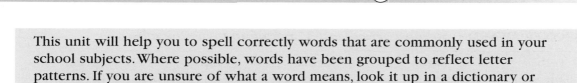

This unit will help you to spell correctly words that are commonly used in your school subjects. Where possible, words have been grouped to reflect letter patterns. If you are unsure of what a word means, look it up in a dictionary or check with your teacher.

Each subject section has three levels: BRONZE, SILVER AND GOLD. Starting with the bronze level, for each section:

1 Get a friend to test your spelling of each word.
2 For each word that you have spelled correctly: WELL DONE! Note down the numbers of the words you have spelled wrongly.
3 Use the strategies in Unit 1 to learn the spellings you got wrong.
4 Get a friend to test you again. If you have spelled enough words correctly to move on to the next level, ask your teacher for an award and start the next level.

Go for GOLD in every subject!

Technology

BRONZE AWARD *(you must get at least 29 out of 30 to get the award)*

1 computer	7 display	13 mouse	19 plan	25 format
2 printer	8 safety	14 surface	20 grain	26 diet
3 scanner	9 pixel	15 force	21 icon	27 brief
4 power	10 mineral	16 scale	22 fashion	28 mass
5 menu	11 tool	17 file	23 vitamin	29 mould
6 logo	12 colour	18 mobile	24 drawing	30 hazard

SILVER AWARD *(you must get at least 26 out of 30 to get the award)*

1 investigation	7 suitability	13 keyboard	19 lathe	25 balanced
2 presentation	8 imperial	14 fibre	20 outcome	26 graphics
3 function	9 industrial	15 centre	21 indicate	27 gluten
4 labelling	10 design	16 pressure	22 criteria	28 protein
5 packaging	11 detail	17 assemble	23 browser	29 preview
6 dyeing	12 document	18 vegetable	24 monitor	30 research

GOLD AWARD *(you must get at least 25 out of 30 to get the award)*

1 specification	7 displacement	13 technological	19 processor	25 efficiency
2 acceleration	8 implement	14 appearance	20 embroidery	26 elasticity
3 evaluation	9 component	15 adjustable	21 auxiliary	27 durability
4 limitations	10 nutrients	16 analyse	22 approximately	28 quantify
5 carbohydrate	11 hydrodynamics	17 specialise	23 inversely	29 diagram
6 laminate	12 aerodynamic	18 temperature	24 buoyancy	30 diffusing

English

BRONZE AWARD *(you must get at least 37 out of 40 to get the award)*

1 verb	9 jargon	17 media	25 rap	33 speech
2 adverb	10 theme	18 drama	26 noun	34 develop
3 sonnet	11 scene	19 jingle	27 scan	35 discuss
4 bracket	12 image	20 riddle	28 pun	36 draft
5 comma	13 write	21 vowel	29 poem	37 inform
6 comment	14 quote	22 capital	30 prose	38 object
7 contrast	15 ode	23 blurb	31 play	39 fact
8 colon	16 argue	24 ballad	32 slang	40 epic

SILVER AWARD *(you must get at least 58 out of 65 to get the award)*

1 fiction	14 irony	27 describe	40 rhyme	53 phrase
2 emotion	15 summary	28 genre	41 narrative	54 accent
3 preposition	16 empathy	29 organise	42 anecdote	55 antonym
4 opinion	17 imply	30 feature	43 article	56 extract
5 question	18 critical	31 fable	44 clause	57 character
6 idiom	19 literal	32 farce	45 simile	58 singular
7 acrostic	20 personal	33 appropriate	46 participle	59 narrator
8 symbolic	21 plural	34 audience	47 paragraph	60 stanza
9 polemic	22 dialect	35 adjective	48 prefix	61 insight
10 tragedy	23 couplet	36 illustrate	49 pronoun	62 limerick
11 parody	24 myth	37 persuade	50 proverb	63 Shakespeare
12 elegy	25 legend	38 language	51 epitaph	64 suffix
13 analogy	26 grammar	39 passage	52 hyphen	65 tabloid

GOLD AWARD *(you must get at least 34 out of 40 to get the award)*

1 abbreviation	9 characteristic	17 dialogue	25 participle	33 euphemism
2 alliteration	10 linguistic	18 monologue	26 palindrome	34 onomatopoeia
3 conjunction	11 allegorical	19 caricature	27 synecdoche	35 enjambment
4 exclamation	12 rhythmical	20 literature	28 soliloquy	36 consonant
5 interjection	13 chronological	21 syllable	29 literacy	37 ambiguous
6 personification	14 rhetorical	22 persuasive	30 autobiography	38 pentameter
7 punctuation	15 haiku	23 homophone	31 synonym	39 metaphor
8 quotation	16 oxymoron	24 phoneme	32 acronym	40 apostrophe

Mathematics

BRONZE AWARD *(you must get at least 42 out of 45 to get the award)*

1 acute	10 factor	19 length	28 pentagon	37 zero
2 cosine	11 area	20 width	29 polygon	38 vertex
3 sine	12 square	21 data	30 wrong	39 convex
4 cube	13 minus	22 angle	31 right	40 add
5 cubic	14 compass	23 total	32 chance	41 mean
6 litre	15 plane	24 equal	33 regular	42 metre
7 similar	16 outcome	25 value	34 locus	43 volume
8 sector	17 sum	26 mode	35 axis	44 scale
9 vector	18 depth	27 degree	36 helix	45 clockwise

SILVER AWARD *(you must get at least 75 out of 85 to get the award)*

1 calculate	18 perimeter	35 deviation	52 significant	69 weight
2 alternate	19 integer	36 reflection	53 graph	70 height
3 coordinate	20 linear	37 dimension	54 sphere	71 ratio
4 collate	21 latitude	38 matrix	55 bearing	72 algebra
5 horizontal	22 longitude	39 concave	56 recurring	73 chord
6 diagonal	23 distribution	40 validity	57 scalene	74 ellipse
7 decimal	24 divide	41 probability	58 rhombus	75 vertices
8 vertical	25 median	42 capacity	59 product	76 histogram
9 triangle	26 decagon	43 frequency	60 measure	77 radius
10 rectangle	27 octagon	44 cylinder	61 gradient	78 average
11 variable	28 heptagon	45 circle	62 tangent	79 converge
12 Celsius	29 hexagon	46 maximum	63 adjacent	80 estimate
13 centre	30 fraction	47 minimum	64 segment	81 digit
14 centimetre	31 rotation	48 relative	65 difference	82 protractor
15 millimetre	32 elevation	49 negative	66 hectare	83 prism
16 kilometre	33 distribution	50 parallel	67 quadratic	84 pyramid
17 diameter	34 inclination	51 inverse	68 isometric	85 obtuse

GOLD AWARD *(you must get at least 29 out of 35 to get the award)*

1 statistical	8 tessellation	15 concentric	22 parabola	29 circumference
2 reciprocal	9 subtraction	16 congruent	23 perpendicular	30 questionnaire
3 geometrical	10 extrapolation	17 quotient	24 denominator	31 complementary
4 equilateral	11 multiplication	18 coefficient	25 cumulative	32 trigonometry
5 quadrilateral	12 octahedron	19 equidistant	26 trapezium	33 isosceles
6 symmetrical	13 dodecagon	20 percentage	27 Pythagoras	34 parallelogram
7 correlation	14 dodecahedron	21 Fahrenheit	28 hypotenuse	35 simultaneous

Science

BRONZE AWARD (*you must get at least 46 out of 50 to get the award*)

1 tube	11 fungus	21 artery	31 alcohol	41 reptile
2 acid	12 focus	22 density	32 extinct	42 blood
3 plasma	13 flame	23 energy	33 exert	43 atom
4 spatula	14 funnel	24 kidney	34 valve	44 proton
5 sensor	15 material	25 molten	35 heart	45 voltage
6 element	16 tripod	26 growth	36 digest	46 hormone
7 pigment	17 joule	27 gas	37 dilute	47 force
8 solvent	18 electron	28 beaker	38 solid	48 spore
9 planet	19 air	29 Petri dish	39 Bunsen	49 tissue
10 alloy	20 vary	30 watt	40 vein	50 lava

SILVER AWARD (*you must get at least 66 out of 75 to get the award*)

1 indicator	16 velocity	31 dispersion	46 hygiene	61 neutron
2 conductor	17 gravity	32 emulsion	47 source	62 corrosive
3 insulator	18 chemistry	33 combustion	48 eclipse	63 atmosphere
4 resistor	19 biology	34 alkaline	49 nucleus	64 medicine
5 transistor	20 astronomy	35 habitat	50 isotope	65 residue
6 ammeter	21 classify	36 periodic	51 pipette	66 muscle
7 polymer	22 refraction	37 genetic	52 membrane	67 apparatus
8 nuclear	23 revolution	38 kinetic	53 microscope	68 optical
9 formula	24 solution	39 soluble	54 physics	69 dissolve
10 bacteria	25 evaporation	40 particle	55 disease	70 organism
11 inertia	26 ovulation	41 molecule	56 structure	71 crystal
12 omnivore	27 reproduction	42 blood	57 oxygen	72 volcano
13 carnivore	28 friction	43 hydrogen	58 skeleton	73 stomach
14 humidity	29 rotation	44 proton	59 experiment	74 catalyst
15 electricity	30 suspension	45 magnetic	60 liquid	75 observation

GOLD AWARD (*you must get at least 29 out of 35 to get the award*)

1 thermometer	8 distillation	15 sedimentary	22 impermeable	29 chlorophyll
2 centrifuge	9 classification	16 laboratory	23 electromagnet	30 radioactive
3 pollination	10 concentration	17 embryonic	24 photosynthesis	31 hemisphere
4 fertilisation	11 environment	18 precipitate	25 electrolysis	32 proportional
5 constellation	12 enzyme	19 invertebrate	26 chromosome	33 menstrual
6 condensation	13 igneous	20 metabolism	27 vaccine	34 haemoglobin
7 germination	14 diaphragm	21 biodegradable	28 chromatography	35 liquefy

Humanities

BRONZE AWARD *(you must get at least 29 out of 30 to get the award)*

1 bible	7 rule	13 snow	19 iceberg	25 waste
2 cause	8 law	14 faith	20 rite	26 map
3 plain	9 Hindu	15 desert	21 flood	27 town
4 rain	10 atlas	16 scale	22 grid	28 valley
5 saint	11 river	17 church	23 fault	29 moral
6 village	12 city	18 gospel	24 vicar	30 pulpit

SILVER AWARD *(you must get at least 71 out of 80 to get the award)*

1 climate	17 irrigation	33 parable	49 continent	65 coniferous
2 country	18 migration	34 reliable	50 judgement	66 tornado
3 industry	19 civilisation	35 festival	51 sediment	67 priest
4 century	20 location	36 feudal	52 Anglican	68 survey
5 primary	21 liberation	37 regional	53 Christian	69 Islam
6 missionary	22 generation	38 glacial	54 ocean	70 mining
7 secondary	23 abortion	39 heaven	55 worship	71 refuge
8 meander	24 condensation	40 monarch	56 fascist	72 suburb
9 founder	25 preservation	41 hurricane	57 racial	73 cyclone
10 Passover	26 erosion	42 Saviour	58 peasant	74 prejudice
11 dictator	27 depression	43 contour	59 typhoon	75 Ordnance
12 weather	28 barbaric	44 fossil	60 prophet	76 Muslim
13 Judaism	29 agnostic	45 developed	61 earthquake	77 decade
14 tourism	30 heretic	46 spirit	62 relief	78 abolish
15 population	31 republic	47 belief	63 communist	79 merciful
16 conurbation	32 miracle	48 settlement	64 prayer	80 services

GOLD AWARD *(you must get at least 34 out of 40 to get the award)*

1 reference	9 reformation	17 Messiah	25 crucify	33 synagogue
2 conscience	10 contraception	18 prejudice	26 propaganda	34 agricultural
3 independence	11 Sikh	19 manufacturing	27 democratic	35 hydrological
4 stalactite	12 blitzkrieg	20 commandment	28 suicide	36 Buddhist
5 stalagmite	13 millennium	21 parliament	29 Pharisee	37 archaeology
6 concentration	14 atheism	22 government	30 tertiary	38 Renaissance
7 secularisation	15 pacifism	23 conclusion	31 tributary	39 carboniferous
8 precipitation	16 euthanasia	24 Mediterranean	32 martyr	40 trilobite

WELL DONE on completing the tests! Check your answers very carefully. Then use the table below each set of answers to find out which part of the book will help you.

Diagnostic test 1: Plurals (page 18)

Check your answers carefully against the correct spelling,

1 phones	11 elves	21 proofs	31 celebrities	41 stimuli
2 wives	12 cigars	22 sundials	32 holidays	42 vetoes
3 parishes	13 geese	23 families	33 handcuffs	43 calves
4 loaves	14 valleys	24 halves	34 churches	44 masses
5 studios	15 countries	25 videos	35 glasses	45 schoolboys
6 policemen	16 chefs	26 buoys	36 televisions	46 watches
7 dummies	17 cacti	27 safes	37 cargoes	47 oases
8 clocks	18 faxes	28 children	38 chiefs	48 alarms
9 temples	19 teeth	29 kilos	39 sheep	49 strays
10 printers	20 monitors	30 phenomena	40 factories	50 aircraft

Now use this table to show which part of Unit 3: Plurals can help you.

Mistakes on numbers:	Unit 3: Section and page	Activities
1, 3, 8, 9, 10, 12, 18, 20, 22, 34, 35, 36, 44, 46, 48	**s** or **es**? p33	1, 2
5, 25, 29, 37, 42	words ending in **o**: p34	1
7, 14, 15, 23, 26, 31, 32, 40, 45, 49	words ending in **y**: p33	1, 2
2, 4, 11, 16, 21, 24, 27, 33, 38, 43	words ending in **f**, **ff** or **fe**: p 32	1, 2
6, 13, 17, 19, 28, 30, 39, 41, 47, 50	no change plurals: p34	2
	irregular plurals: p35 foreign words: p35	1, 2, 3 2, 3

Test 2: Spelling and punctuation

Diagnostic test 2: Spelling and punctuation

Check your answers carefully against the correct punctuation.

1 The boy asked, 'Is it Monday today, Joe?'
2 'My make-up is running,' cried Andrea.
3 We don't know what he did with Sam's shoes.
4 The girls' changing rooms were left in a terrible mess.
5 I think I would like to work for the RSPCA.
6 Julie and Richard went to Spain at Easter.
7 You and I should watch Friends on TV tonight.
8 I'm going to do a lot of work today.
9 I'm going to Pete's after school. You'll miss out if you don't come.
10 Almost everyone thinks the treasure is inside the pyramid.
11 He has spent a record-breaking amount of time in the reserves.
12 Jane said, 'You really should learn to spell properly.'
13 You're all daft if you're going there. We're staying right here.
14 The dog's going crazy, it'll bite you.
15 'The motorway was a bit busy this morning,' said Alan.

Now use this table to show which part of Unit 7: Spelling and punctuation can help you.

Mistakes on numbers:	Unit 7: Section and page	Activities
1, 5, 6, 7, 12	Capital letters pages 81-82	1, 2, 3
2, 11	Hyphens page 86	1, 2
3, 9, 13, 14	Apostrophes of abbreviation page 83 (See also Using apostrophes correctly page 31)	1, 2
4	Apostrophes of possession pages 84-85	1, 2
8, 10, 15	How many words? page 87	1, 2

Test 3: Unusual features of spelling: answers

Diagnostic test 3: Homophones, silent letters, Americanisms, deliberate misspelling

Check your answers very carefully.

---

1 It's **plain** to see that everyone is **here** now.
2 I **honestly** think I've **wrecked** my **knuckles**; I think they're broken.
3 I'm not sure **whether** he was **bored** or not.
4 I'm in your **debt** because you cured my **pneumonia**.
5 The plate will **break** if it falls **off** the table.
6 Have you **seen** the park? The circus is **there** this **week**.
7 Which **colour** would you like? Orange, **grey** or blue?
8 I **know** that I need **to** work hard on my spelling.
9 I didn't **realise** your **behaviour** could be so awful.
10 It's because I'm **crazy** that I'm going to give **you** my money.
11 Did we win or **lose** the 400 **metres** relay?
12 It would be **easy** to take the **quick** route.

Now use this table to show which part of Unit 8: Misc-spell-aneous can help you.

Mistakes on numbers:	Unit 8: Section and page	Activities
1, 3, 5, 6, 8, 11	Homophones pages 90–94	1, 2, 3, 4, 5, 6, 7, 8, 9, 10
2, 4	Silent letters page 95	1, 2
10, 12	Deliberate misspelling page 96	1
7, 9	Americanisms page 97	1

Test 4: Soft letter sounds: answers

Diagnostic test 4: soft letter sounds

Check your answers very carefully against the correct spelling.

1 face	7 bilge	13 place	19 surgeon	25 agency
2 palace	8 cigar	14 furnace	20 pencil	26 symmetry
3 genius	9 mice	15 city	21 large	27 range
4 cylinder	10 bliss	16 hiss	22 bridge	28 incinerator
5 poultice	11 sauce	17 single	23 damage	29 symbol
6 massive	12 mouse	18 jewel	24 justice	30 giraffe

Now use this table to show which part of Unit 5: Common letter patterns can help you.

Mistakes on numbers:	Unit 5: Section and page	Activities
1, 6, 11, 12, 13	Soft 'c' spellings pages 50–51	1, 2
5, 10, 16, 24	'-ice' or '-iss' endings page 51	3
2, 14	'-ace' endings page 51	4
4, 8, 9, 15, 17, 20, 25, 26, 28, 29	Soft 'cy' and 'ci' spellings page 52	1, 2
3, 7, 18, 19, 27, 30	Soft and hard letters page 50 Soft 'g' spellings page 50	1
21, 22, 23	'-ge' and '-dge' endings page 54	1, 2, 3

Tests 5 and 6: Common letter patterns: answers

Diagnostic test 5: Common letter patterns
Check your answer carefully against the correct choice.

1 vein	7 future	13 typhoon	19 shield	25 graphic
2 science	8 ancient	14 weight	20 grieve	26 freight
3 piece	9 believe	15 species	21 stuffing	27 field
4 ceiling	10 triumph	16 deceive	22 gruff	28 hurried
5 photocopier	11 weird	17 orphan	23 thieves	29 view
6 agencies	12 society	18 their	24 fancied	30 reprieve

Now use this table to show which part of Unit 5: Common letter patterns can help you.

Mistakes on numbers:	Unit 5: Section and page	Activities
5, 7, 10, 13, 17, 21, 22, 25	'ph' words page 55	1, 2
3, 4, 9, 11, 16, 19, 20, 23, 27, 28, 29, 30	'ei' or 'ie' spellings? page 56	1, 2
1, 14, 18, 26	'ei' words page 57	3, 4
6, 24	Danger box page 57, Adding a suffix: 'y' becomes 'ie'	
8, 15	Danger box page 57, 'cie' words	
2, 12	Danger box page 57, Two separate sounds	

Diagnostic test 6: Common letter patterns
Check your answer carefully against the correct choice.

1 echo	10 cushion	19 charade	28 courage	37 opaque
2 patch	11 rich	20 wretched	29 plump	38 fake
3 church	12 what	21 sketching	30 cloud	39 question
4 courage	13 squabble	22 monarch	31 shower	40 was
5 growl	14 young	23 brusque	32 warden	41 chemical
6 brochure	15 quality	24 chandelier	33 warp	42 catching
7 which	16 warble	25 shandy	34 switch	43 qualify
8 attach	17 count	26 hutch	35 ditch	44 spouse
9 clout	18 brown	27 much	36 technical	45 require

Now use this table to show which part of Unit 5: Common letter patterns can help you.

Mistakes on numbers:	Unit 5: Section and page	Activities
2, 3, 7, 8, 11, 20, 21, 26, 27, 34, 35, 42	'tch' and 'ch' words page 58	1, 2
6, 10, 19, 24, 25	'ch' or 'sh' words page 59	1
1, 22, 36, 41	'ch' or 'k' words page 59	2, 3
5, 9, 17, 18, 30, 31, 44	'ou' and 'ow' sounding the same page 60	1
4, 14, 28, 29	'ou' and 'u' sounding the same page 60	2
12, 16, 32, 33, 40	'w' letter patterns page 61	1, 2, 3
13, 15, 23, 37, 38, 39, 43, 45	'q' letter patterns page 62	1, 2, 3

Diagnostic test 7: Prefixes and suffixes: answers

Diagnostic test 7: Prefixes and suffixes
Check your answers against the correct options.

1 unknown	11 friendship	21 although
2 underground	12 brightest	22 misbehave
3 preview	13 mixing	23 unnatural
4 impossible	14 involvement	24 illegal
5 misbehave	15 useless	25 misspent
6 overhead	16 sharpen	26 overrule
7 misspell	17 destroyed	27 immature
8 unnecessary	18 lower	28 unnoticed
9 antidote	19 darkness	29 irregular
10 disagree	20 reported	30 immediate

31 darkness	41 attractiveness	51 marrying
32 brightly	42 ladies	52 abilities
33 appointment	43 amused	53 slobbish
34 pointed	44 playfully	54 wetter
35 interesting	45 forgiving	55 cancelling
36 tuneful	46 heaviest	56 travelling
37 exactly	47 priceless	57 careless
38 kindest	48 nursing	58 hopeful
39 forgiveness	49 sharpest	59 controlling
40 carrying	50 forced	60 spiralling

Now use this table to show which part of Unit 4: Prefixes and suffixes can help you.

Mistakes on numbers:	Unit 4: Section and page	Activities
1–10	Prefixes pages 37–39	1, 2, 3, 4
11–20	Suffixes page 40	1, 2
21–30	Prefixes pages 37–39	1, 2, 3, 4
31–40	Suffixes page 40	1, 2
41, 43, 45, 47, 48, 50	When to keep 'e'/when to drop 'e' pages 42–43	1, 2, 3, 4
42, 46, 52	Changing 'y' to 'i' page 47	1, 2
53, 54	Doubling pages 44–45	1, 2, 3, 4
49, 57, 58	Suffixes page 40	1, 2
55, 56, 59, 60	'l' rule page 46	1, 2
44, 51	Changing 'y' to 'i' page 47	1, 2

Diagnostic test 8: Word endings

Diagnostic test 8: Word endings
Check your answers very carefully against the correct options.

1 televi<u>sion</u>	7 ver<u>sion</u>	13 progre<u>ssion</u>	19 opti<u>cian</u>
2 magi<u>cian</u>	8 techni<u>cian</u>	14 distrib<u>ution</u>	20 ac<u>tion</u>
3 adora<u>tion</u>	9 profe<u>ssion</u>	15 confe<u>ssion</u>	21 politi<u>cian</u>
4 admi<u>ssion</u>	10 vi<u>sion</u>	16 electri<u>cian</u>	22 po<u>tion</u>
5 expre<u>ssion</u>	11 aggre<u>ssion</u>	17 musi<u>cian</u>	23 explo<u>sion</u>
6 revi<u>sion</u>	12 emo<u>tion</u>	18 occa<u>sion</u>	24 promo<u>tion</u>

25 fabul<u>ous</u>	30 advanta<u>geous</u>	35 hide<u>ous</u>	40 mysteri<u>ous</u>
26 seri<u>ous</u>	31 caut<u>ious</u>	36 ambit<u>ious</u>	41 simultan<u>eous</u>
27 gener<u>ous</u>	32 marvell<u>ous</u>	37 gorg<u>eous</u>	42 spontan<u>eous</u>
28 coura<u>geous</u>	33 nerv<u>ous</u>	38 fam<u>ous</u>	
29 superstit<u>ious</u>	34 obv<u>ious</u>	39 danger<u>ous</u>	

43 decim<u>al</u>	49 surviv<u>al</u>	55 residenti<u>al</u>	61 dimp<u>le</u>
44 manu<u>al</u>	50 person<u>al</u>	56 memori<u>al</u>	62 fidd<u>le</u>
45 purp<u>le</u>	51 mudd<u>le</u>	57 materi<u>al</u>	63 crad<u>le</u>
46 bott<u>le</u>	52 miner<u>al</u>	58 stubb<u>le</u>	64 funer<u>al</u>
47 fin<u>al</u>	53 comic<u>al</u>	59 mirac<u>le</u>	65 sensib<u>le</u>
48 bubb<u>le</u>	54 emotion<u>al</u>	60 critic<u>al</u>	66 benefici<u>al</u>

67 indic<u>ate</u>	72 irrit<u>ate</u>	77 imperson<u>ate</u>	82 navig<u>ate</u>
68 favour<u>ite</u>	73 oppos<u>ite</u>	78 celebr<u>ate</u>	83 evapor<u>ate</u>
69 narr<u>ate</u>	74 complic<u>ate</u>	79 altern<u>ate</u>	84 demonstr<u>ate</u>
70 anim<u>ate</u>	75 est<u>ate</u>	80 co-oper<u>ate</u>	
71 gran<u>ite</u>	76 defin<u>ite</u>	81 particip<u>ate</u>	

85 physi<u>cal</u>	90 art<u>icle</u>	95 part<u>icle</u>	100 chemi<u>cal</u>
86 magi<u>cal</u>	91 ic<u>icle</u>	96 musi<u>cal</u>	101 spect<u>acle</u>
87 cub<u>icle</u>	92 practi<u>cal</u>	97 bibli<u>cal</u>	102 classi<u>cal</u>
88 veh<u>icle</u>	93 tent<u>acle</u>	98 mir<u>acle</u>	
89 astrologi<u>cal</u>	94 logi<u>cal</u>	99 verti<u>cal</u>	

103 lic<u>ence</u>	107 excell<u>ence</u>	111 appli<u>ance</u>	115 experi<u>ence</u>
104 insur<u>ance</u>	108 disturb<u>ance</u>	112 sci<u>ence</u>	116 perform<u>ance</u>
105 resid<u>ence</u>	109 coincid<u>ence</u>	113 ambul<u>ance</u>	117 rom<u>ance</u>
106 sent<u>ence</u>	110 brilli<u>ance</u>	114 audi<u>ence</u>	118 depend<u>ence</u>

Diagnostic test 9: Letter patterns

Now use this table to show which part of Unit 6: Common endings can help you.

Mistakes on numbers:	Unit 6: Section and page	Activities
1, 6, 7, 10, 18, 23	'-sion' endings page 71	2, 3
3, 12, 14, 20, 22, 24	'-tion' endings page 69	1, 2
4, 5, 9, 11, 13, 15	'-ssion' endings page 70	1, 2
2, 8, 16, 17, 19, 21	'-cian' and '-sion' endings page 71	1, 2, 3
25, 27, 32, 33, 38, 39	'-ous' endings page 67	1, 2
26, 29, 31, 34, 36, 40	'-ious- endings page 68	1, 2
28, 30, 35, 37, 41, 42	'-eous' endings page 68	3
45, 46, 48, 51, 58, 59, 61, 62, 63, 65	'-le' endings page 72	1
43, 44, 47, 49, 50, 52, 53, 54, 55, 56, 57, 60, 64, 66	'al' endings page 73	1, 2
67, 68, 69, 70, 71, 72, 73, 74, 75, 76, 77, 78, 79, 80, 81, 82, 83, 84	'-ate' or '-ite' endings page 78	1, 2, 3
85, 86, 89, 92, 94, 96, 97, 99, 100, 102	'-ical' endings page 75	1
87, 88, 90, 91, 93, 95, 98, 101	'-icle' and '-acle' endings page 76	1, 2
103, 104, 105, 106, 107, 108, 109, 110, 111, 112, 113, 114, 115, 116, 117, 118	'-ance' and '-ence' endings page 77	1, 2

Diagnostic test 9: Letter patterns

Check your answers very carefully against the correct letter patterns.

1 pain	10 ceiling	19 dye	28 dough	37 pupil
2 always	11 believe	20 lie	29 lose	38 tune
3 obey	12 treat	21 type	30 June	39 few
4 weighty	13 street	22 road	31 rude	40 ewe
5 great	14 machine	23 own	32 spoon	41 neutral
6 danger	15 bite	24 slow	33 crew	42 Europe
7 break	16 eye	25 bones	34 shampoo	
8 scream	17 goodbye	26 boat	35 computer	
9 complete	18 buy	27 sew	36 Tuesday	

Use this table to show which part of Unit 2: Vowels and consonants can help you.

Mistakes on numbers:	Unit 2: Section and page	Activities
1, 2, 3, 4, 5, 6, 7	Long vowel sound 'a' page 26	1, 2, 3
8, 9, 10, 11, 12, 13, 14	Long vowel sound 'e' page 27	1, 2
15, 16, 17, 18, 19, 20, 21	Long vowel sound 'i' page 27	3, 4
22, 23, 24, 25, 26, 27, 28	Long vowel sound 'o' page 28	1
29, 30, 31, 32, 33, 34	Long vowel sound 'u' page 28	2
35, 36, 37, 38, 39, 40, 41, 42	Long vowel sound 'u' page 28	2

Glossary

Abbreviation	A word written in a shortened form. For example: **don't** is an abbreviation of **do not**.
Adjective	A word that describes something. For example: huge, lonely, smelly.
Breve	A curly mark above a letter that indicates a short vowel sound. The opposite of a macron. For example: bĭg, cŭt, tĕnnis.
Consonant	All the letters of the alphabet apart from the vowels.
Consonant suffix	A suffix which starts with a consonant. For example: -**ness**.
Compound words	When two or more separate root words are put together. For example: **Foot + ball = football.**
Drafting	The process of checking and proof-reading work to improve it and correct mistakes.
Homophone	Words that sound the same but have different spellings and meanings. For example: **cereal / serial allowed / aloud.**
Infinitive	The most basic form of a verb, with 'to' in front of it. For example: to play, to be, to run.
Irregular plurals	Plurals that are not formed by adding **s**, or letter combinations including **s**. For example: **child → children.**
Macron	A short line placed over a letter to indicate a long vowel sound. Opposite of a breve. For example: dānger, tūne, bīte.
Mnemonic	A rhyme or saying to help you remember a spelling. For exmple: Sep**arat**e is **a rat** of a word.
Noun	A word that names things. For example: car, worry, table, life.
Plural	A word that indicates there is more than one. For example: cows, pennies, knives.
Pronoun	A word used instead of a noun. For example: it, he, she, we, they.
Proper noun	A noun which names something specific. For example: Andrew, France, Eastenders. Proper nouns always have a capital letter.
Prefix	A group of letters added to the beginning of a word which changes the meaning. For example: **Mis** + understand = misunderstand.
Root	A word to which prefixes and suffixes may be added to make other words. For example, with unclear, cleared or clearly, the root word is clear. It is sometimes called a stem word.
Silent letter	Letters that appear in the spelling of a word but are not heard when the word is spoken: For example: dum**b**, **k**nee, **w**rong.
Singular	A word that indicates there is only one of something. For example: cow, penny, knife.
Suffix	A group of letters added to the end of a word which changes the meaning. Understand + **ing** = understanding.
Syllable	Each separate beat or sound in a word. For example: chapter = 2 syllables (**chap + ter**); forgotten = 3 syllables (**for + got + ten**).
Verb	An action or 'doing' word. For example: frown, punch, stretch, eat.
Vowel	The letters **a**, **e**, **i**, **o**, **u** are all vowels. **Y** can also be used as a vowel.
Vowel suffix	A word ending which starts with a vowel. For example: -**ing**.